THE INS & OUTS:

PERFECTING THE QUILTING STITCH

DEDICATION

To Bill

THE INS & OUTS:

PERFECTING THE QUILTING STITCH

PATRICIA J. MORRIS

American Quilter's Society

P. O. Box 3290 • Paducah, KY 42002-3290

ACKNOWLEDGMENTS

My gratitude to Diane Neff for helping to realize in her illustrations ideas from the text and to George Neff for his artistic advice.

I also acknowledge the help of my husband, Bill, who not only suffered through my writing of this book that consumed so much of our time together, but also read and commented on each page from the standpoint of the general reader.

And, finally, I thank all my students, quilting colleagues and friends who, individually and collectively, have contributed to my awareness of the Ins and Outs.

TABLE OF CONTENTS

INTRODUCTION

We call what we do "quilting" but sometimes actual quilting – the execution of small, even stitches that hold together the three layers of the quilt and provide an additional design element to the work – seems to be the least important of what we do. Of the three basic techniques usually associated with quiltmaking – piecing, applique, and quilting – quilting is the technique that seems to have received little attention over the years.

There are an infinite number of patterns for piecing and applique. Detailed instructions for executing piecing and applique are found everywhere. Whether it's hand or machine piecing, quick piecing, or any other type or variation, instructions abound. Applique, reverse applique, machine applique and other types are detailed in many sources. But usually the instructions on quilting tell you to baste the textile sandwich and quilt, with little information beyond that. There are patterns for quilting designs available but not nearly the number available for the other two basic techniques.

And tops awaiting quilting abound. Unquilted tops are stored in attics, sold in shops, and hoarded by today's quiltmakers. Our ancestors seem to have made more quilt tops than they ever managed to get quilted. And today, if you talk to a quiltmaker working on a new quilt top, you're almost certain to discover that that person has a few completed tops tucked away waiting to be quilted while progress starts on yet another top. Yes, we do seem to think and talk about quilting more than we do it.

There are many reasons that could explain the phenomenon of unquilted projects. After all, piecing and applique work are more portable than quilting. These techniques can also be done in snatches of time here and there. They are less bulky to work with. Piecing and applique work can be done with scraps of leftover fabric, while quilting involves a relatively larger investment at one time in backing fabric and batting.

Piecing and applique work can be thought of in small bits. You can start to piece or applique a single block knowing that it will be completed in a short time and then you can start to piece or applique the next one. And soon you'll have enough blocks set together into a top. But once the textile sandwich has been basted, you are faced with a large, single task, that of quilting the project. You are stuck with an immense job and you know it's going to take a big chunk of time to complete it. And now you can no longer physically tackle it bit by bit: no matter how often you think of it as quilting one area, then another area, it has turned into a singular, sometimes overwhelming challenge.

Patterns for piecing and applique can be passed from hand to hand and most people grasp the idea and execute the technique without a great deal of difficulty. At some point, they have sewn two pieces of fabric together or put a patch on top of another piece of fabric. But being shown a quilting pattern is like being spoken to in a foreign language; there's no point of reference. The usual way of learning the quilting technique has been to watch it being done or to work alongside an accomplished quiltmaker, thereby gaining skill through experience.

A thorough investigation of the quilting technique would help break down the mystique surrounding it. And that is the aim of this book. Knowing how to quilt and how to approach the quilting should help the novice gain confidence and skill. It should go a long way toward taking away the reluctance to begin on the huge, but inevitable, task of quilting a project.

This book, then, will attempt a thorough investigation of the quilting technique, what it is, how it's done and what factors can affect it. The purpose is to help quiltmakers, both new and experienced, to perfect the quilting stitch and its use.

THE QUILTING DESIGN

When you think about quilting a project, you have to start somewhere and the quilting design is a logical place to start. Just what kind of a design do you want to use for a given top? The most important thing to keep in mind is that the quilting design needs to be as carefully planned as the quilt top itself.

Once the project has been quilted and you look at it, remember that you will be viewing the spaces and shadows created by the quilting stitches themselves. Your view of a quilt, unless you have extraordinary eyesight, is not of a series of quilting stitches on the quilt, but the results of these stitches. Once again: the results of the stitches are the spaces and shadows and the texturing that appears. These spaces and shadows form the additional and final design element of your quilt. Quilting is the last chance the quiltmaker has to communicate with the viewer. And while it is the final design element the quiltmaker adds to the quilt, it is one of the first elements that the quilt viewer takes in. These spaces and shadows created by the quilting are present in all types of quilts, whether pieced, appliqued, whole cloth or the results of some other technique.

The quilting design should work with the top design to create an integrated work. It is true that the makers of older quilts used quilting primarily to hold the three layers together without much thought about the relationship between the top design and the quilting design. This was necessary in order to have enough quilting to keep the layers together and the batting in place. Many older quilts are truly beautiful and works of art in their own right. However, a quilting design that works with the top design, rather than merely being superimposed on it, can improve any top. Modern thinking is that the quilting design should be planned to enhance and highlight the top design and modern materials allow the quilters a far wider range of possibilities. The quilting design can bring forward to the viewer's attention any of the elements the maker wants to focus on, and, by the same token, can make recede or make less focal any element the maker chooses. Quilting can work with the top colors to make them more visible or less visible or cause them to act together in different ways by adding or reducing the focus on them.

A quilting design worked in any given open area is best if it doesn't stand alone. Frequently a quilt top, especially an appliqued quilt top, is set together using alternate blocks. Every other block is a design block and the alternate blocks are solid pieces of fabric. A design quilted in an alternate block may look nice while the quilt is in your hand, but back away a little and you'll find this design may tend to vanish. What is needed is background quilting (something as simple as crossing diagonal lines entirely surrounding the quilted design) to support it.

Background quilting is especially important in whole-cloth quilts. Whole-cloth quilts are solid pieces of fabric with quilting being the only design and technical element employed. They are also referred to as white-on-white quilts. Prove the value of background quilting to yourself by quilting a double heart on a small whole-cloth pillow top. This double heart may look nice, but there will likely be a great deal of unsecured open area around it. Now support this quilted double heart by adding background quilting. The background quilting will sink the unsecured open area and your quilted open heart will come forward, show up better, and look nicer than when it stood alone. Technically, it will also hold the three layers together more securely. So when planning the quilting design, remember to plan for the background quilting you need. The type of background quilting may vary according to the needs for a given quilt, but if your imagination fails at this point, you can be relatively safe by adding the aforementioned crossing diagonal lines to form the background support quilting.

The finished appearance of the quilt is not only affected by the type of quilting design but also by the amount of quilting. The more quilting there is in any given design, the flatter the finished appearance of the work will be. The less quilting there is in any given design, the puffier the finished appearance of the work. The quiltmaker must decide which of these finished appearances is desired or acceptable. The flat versus puffy finished appearance is, of course, relative. I am not talking about quilting so heavy that the design elements of the top are lost or so light that what results is the look of a down comforter. Ideally, the amount of quilting on a given project should be a design decision and not a matter of, "It's gotta be done by next month." This rush-to-completion approach can result in an overly puffy look from an inadequate amount of quilting.

As to where you get quilting designs to use on the quilt top, the answer (most unhelpfully) is everywhere. Look up, down and all around and you'll find yourself inundated with design possibilities. Of course there are concrete sources for quilting designs, such as books (see page 96 for a list of quilting design books). Quilting periodicals regularly publish designs. Pattern designers make them available themselves. Many times you'll also find wonderful quilting designs on old quilts. Be sure you have a sketch pad and pencil (not pen) when you go to shows featuring antique quilts.

But, the best source of inspiration for any given quilt is the quilt top itself. Look at the top, study it, squint at it, secure it to a wall in an area you walk by often. You'll learn which areas you want to highlight and emphasize and which you want to give less focus. Sketch the top design in color on a piece of paper. Overlay the sketch with tracing paper and draw quilting lines on the tracing paper. You'll find what designs will and won't work on your top.

Various other factors will also come into play as you decide on your quilting design and the amount of time you will spend on the quilting. The degree of difficulty of the quilting design will affect the amount of time required to do the quilting. The design can range from single straight lines to elaborate feathered wreaths. A very difficult quilting design can become discouraging to the inexperienced quilter. On the other hand, a very simple design with few challenges can quickly bore you. Try to choose a design with enough challenge that you won't be bored, but a design that is not so difficult or complicated you'll despair of ever completing it and just give up.

The ease of execution of the quilting design is tied to its degree of difficulty, but it is also linked to other factors including the types of fabrics and the kind of batting you are using. These factors will be fully discussed later.

When choosing a design you feel will work with your quilt top, be sure you also *like* the design. If the quilting design is not pleasing to you or if you don't find it interesting or challenging, it can become tedious and unsatisfying to quilt. And you will find that if the design isn't pleasing to you as you quilt it, the quilting will wind up being much more time consuming. It will become the chore you always feared it would be.

You should plan the amount of quilting in all the areas of your quilt to be evenly balanced so that the completed project will lie flat. This is a consideration when choosing a quilting design for any quilt. It is especially important for sampler quilts, medallion quilts, and any quilt where the top pattern varies widely from one area to another. Remember that the quilting "takes up" the area in which it is done. If the amount of quilting is not evenly balanced, the "take up" will vary from area to area, causing the completed quilt to bubble, or ripple in some places or to have edges that are not straight.

Of course, when choosing a quilting design that will complement a pieced or appliqued quilt top you have some basic technique choices that have to be reconciled with the aesthetic decisions. The basic technique choice you must make before planning the entire design is exactly where to put your quilting stitches. On a pieced quilt, you can quilt one-quarter inch away from the seam line and parallel to the seam line. This will give a traditional look to the finished project. Or you can quilt "in the ditch," right along the seam line on the side of the seam where there are no seam allowances. This approach will result in a more modern look to the finished project.

Generally speaking, it's not a good idea to quilt parallel to the seam line and close to it (say one-eighth inch away) on the side where the seam allowances are pressed. While it is possible to do this and for design purposes it may be desirable to do so, it is not easy to execute stitches and control their size when you are quilting through five layers. Naturally, as you quilt you will occasionally cross a seam line and the seam allowances. The one or two stitches needed to cross this area you can usually manage without too much difficulty, but to steadily quilt through five layers can be self-defeating because of the sheer physical difficulty of pushing and pulling the needle through these layers. Why hamper yourself with this additional technical problem?

On an appliqued quilt, the first row of quilting stitches is usually placed on the background as close as possible to the outside edges of the appliqued pieces. Additional quilting is then done on the block, repeating the outline,

adding background quilting or doing whatever else the maker chooses. If the applique piece is large and, because of its size or the type of design, it requires quilting on it, you can cut away the background under the applique before assembling the textile sandwich. This will eliminate the need to quilt through that extra layer of fabric.

Let's say that at this point you have made a decision on your quilting design based on the foregoing guidelines. The stitches are arranged so that the resultant spaces and shadows work with the top design, enhancing and highlighting it so as to present a complete integrated work. Your background quilting is planned and you have decided just how flat or puffy the quilt will be when finished. You've decided the design isn't too easy or difficult, and can be executed given the fabrics and batting you're working with and you feel that it pleases you. You've decided that the amount of quilting you're using will be evenly balanced, and you know just where your stitches will fall. Now it's time to prepare that quilting design for use.

TEMPLATES AND STENCILS

You will now need to make a template or stencil to reproduce the quilting design you've chosen. If the design is from a source other than your imagination, it may be necessary to make some adjustments. You may need to add or eliminate a detail so that the design will fit in a certain area. Once your pattern is drawn on paper with any necessary adjustments, transfer the design to the chosen template or stencil material. To make a lasting tool, use clear or "foggy" plastic for a template or stencil. Medium-weight poster board is also satisfactory, although not as long lasting as plastic.

If you use plastic, lay the plastic on top of the pattern and trace it. If you are using poster board, place carbon paper or transfer paper on top of the poster board, place your pattern on top of that and firmly trace over the lines on the pattern to transfer it.

If you are making a template, cut it from the chosen materials with scissors (utility scissors, not fabric scissors) or a hobby knife. Be sure your cutting instrument is sharp and use it with care to avoid damaging surfaces or cutting yourself.

When you are cutting with scissors, it is often difficult to see your cutting line so you can cut along its inside edge because the scissors blade is in your line of vision when you hold the material in the usual way (Fig. 1A). The usual way is to hold the template in your left hand and cut away the scrap with the scissors held in the right hand. I would suggest you learn a new way of holding the material while you are cutting. Instead of holding the template part in your hand and cutting away the scrap, try holding the scrap in your hand and cutting away the template (Fig. 1B). You will be able to see your line and you'll get a more carefully cut and exact template. It can make all the difference in getting

FIG. 1A

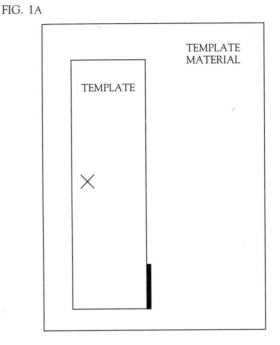

FIG. 1B

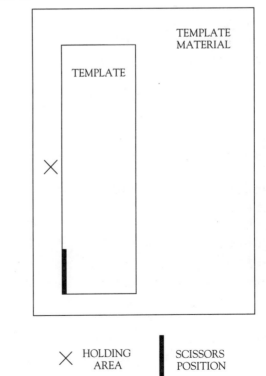

 HOLDING AREA   SCISSORS POSITION

FIG. 2

accurate templates for quilting as well as for piecing and applique.

If you are cutting a stencil, be sure you have a firm cutting surface under the drawn stencil. Cut it with a standard hobby knife, a double-bladed cutting tool, or a burning tool. The most important thing to remember when cutting a stencil is to leave some uncut areas in place to hold the stencil together. Think back to when as a child you cut a snowflake out of folded paper: one cut too many and suddenly you had paper scraps instead of snowflakes. The same principle applies here. Uncut areas must remain if the stencil is to remain whole (Fig. 2).

Although there are many details to consider when choosing a quilting design and making your template or stencil of the design, you don't have to write up a checklist of the guidelines as you make your quilting design decisions. Just keep the list in the back of your mind as you work toward your design. Remember that the most important factor governing your choice of a quilting design is that it should work with your top design to present an integrated example of the quiltmaker's art.

FABRIC

The major component of any quilt is fabric, and in today's marketplace there is a wide range of fabrics available to the quiltmaker. The traditional fabric used for quiltmaking has been cotton. However, this does not mean that the quiltmaker is restricted to its use. Many quiltmakers choose to use blends instead of cottons or in combination with cottons. Probably one of the main reasons for using blends is to get a particular color or print unavailable in cotton. It is possible, of course, to use other types of fabrics in quiltmaking, particularly for wallhangings that don't receive the wear that a bed quilt does.

Overall, I prefer to use cottons and I recommend the use of them. Cottons do not fray as easily as blends and are more workable; they can be eased into place more easily when you are piecing than blends can. Cottons also hold a crease better than blends, thus making applique work go more smoothly.

In regard to the quilting of a project, it is easier to quilt through cotton fabrics than through blends. Blends are more difficult to penetrate and they dull needles more quickly.

The fabric you choose for your project should be able to be quilted with relative ease. The only effective way to test the quiltability of a fabric is to use some of it with the batting you will be using. No amount of theorizing can beat the practical approach of doing a practice piece to see if the fabric needles well.

Consideration also must be given to the intended use of the project and choosing a fabric that is compatible with the intended use. For instance, a particular piece of brocade may needle well and be the perfect fabric touch for a pictorial wallhanging. However, the brocade would probably be a ludicrous choice for a quilt made for a baby's crib.

Another point to consider when choosing a fabric is its weave since the weave can affect the quality of the quilting stitches. A tightly woven fabric is very difficult to quilt through, and the resultant stitches may not be very attractive. Just as a tightly woven fabric may present one particular kind of problem, a loosely woven fabric requires slightly larger quilting stitches than usual to be visually effective because part of each stitch tends to remain sunken in the fibers of the cloth.

The careful use of regularly patterned fabric is also important. Regularly patterned fabric is any fabric that has a dot, stripe or check that repeats uniformly. There are also print fabrics which at first glance appear to be irregular overall, what is usually termed "calico" today. Often just looking at a bolt of the fabric on the shelf in the fabric shop, you assume that it is irregular and therefore easily used. Be sure to unwrap about a yard from the bolt and step back from it to see whether it is really regularly patterned.

Where relatively large portions of a regularly patterned fabric are used, as for example for borders, it becomes more vital than ever to cut the fabric in relation to the pattern as the pattern is now visible over a long stretch of the quilt. If you've ever looked at a quilt that has printed fabric in the border and it looks as if the border is twisted or slightly drunken, chances are that the regularly patterned print fabric was not carefully cut.

When one looks at a quilt, the top contains the most important, most visible use of the fabric. But that doesn't mean that the backing of the quilt can be given less attention. If a print backing is used, it should not shadow through the top as splotches or blotches. This can easily happen when the quilt top is light and the backing has a strong color print or pattern.

If a solid colored backing is used, it should not be so dark as to shadow through the top and alter the color of it (unless this result is desired). For instance, if a quilt top is made of white, light blue solid and light blue prints and perhaps sashed or bordered in a navy blue, it might seem a good idea to use the navy blue as a backing fabric. You'll find that this will make the whole quilt top appear darker. The white will appear to have a blue cast, and the light blue solids and prints will appear a darker blue. If this is the result you want, go ahead and use the navy blue backing. But, if you want the colors for the top to remain as chosen, don't use the navy blue backing. To avoid any problems or surprises of this kind, a rule of thumb to keep in mind is that the color of the quilt top won't be altered if the color for the backing is no darker than the lightest color used in the top. Such a fabric may not be the most exciting backing fabric you can chose, but it will be "safe."

When choosing a backing for a quilt there is a great temptation to use a large piece of fabric that won't require seaming. The obvious temptation in this case is to use a sheet if you can't find commercial quilt backing or extra wide fabric. However, in the best interest of your finished project, try to resist this temptation. A sheet (depending on the type) can have a very high thread count and therefore be difficult to penetrate with a needle. It is usually very hard to pop a knot through a sheet, something you will need to be able to do as you quilt. When using a sheet for a backing you may find that instead of having thread going in and out of fabric, it will look as if you have tiny holes in the sheet with the thread going in and out of the tiny holes. This will not present an attractive quilted look. Also a sheet, particularly a white sheet, never looks totally clean after it is quilted. It often seems to have a slightly dirty cast to it no matter how much you wash it.

If a sheet is not desirable, what next? Of course, muslin is the traditional backing fabric. It is extremely easy to quilt through and will work with almost any batting or top fabric. It is also relatively inexpensive. Most often it requires seaming, but it is superior to a sheet in both finished look and quilting ease. So when you can't come to a decision on a fabric to use for a backing, you know you can't go too far wrong by using muslin. Again, this may not be the best choice, but is a safe choice.

More and more quiltmakers are experimenting with quilt backing, and these experiments have resulted in some exciting design departures. In some cases the entire back is really a second quilt, making the work completely reversible. In other cases the backing is composed of lengths/widths of various fabrics which add interest to the completed work. So, don't restrict yourself to thinking that the backing must be one solid piece of fabric. Remember that the backing can also be a place to try some quilt adventuring.

An extremely important factor to keep in mind when choosing fabric for a quilt backing is that the quality of the backing fabric should be comparable to the quality of the fabrics used in the top. Of course, the amount of fabric needed for a backing can involve quite a sum of money, but it's better to "clobber the piggy bank" and pay the price than to use a cheaper backing fabric. A poor quality backing will shorten the life of the completed project because the quilt will not wear well over time. Also, the quilting stitches will not catch as well on a loosely woven fabric, and the three layers will therefore be less securely anchored together. The use of poor quality backing can seriously detract from your quilt.

In fact, the quality of the fabrics used for the entire project is very important. Considering all of the time, effort, and money involved in making a quilt, it seems foolish to work with anything except good quality fabrics.

FABRIC PREPARATION

Once you have chosen and purchased the fabrics for your quilt, you can't plunge right into the making of it. The fabric must be prepared for use.

The first step in fabric preparation is to wash the material, more than once if necessary. Washing can remove any extra dye that could run. Very bright or very dark fabrics may require more than one washing before the color stops running. In washing fabrics, I use the following procedures.

Each color of fabric is washed individually with detergent, a warm water wash, and a cold rinse. Then, it is washed a second time with a warm water wash and a cold rinse but with no detergent. For this second washing, a white towel is put in with the fabric. I'm very careful to use a towel that won't deposit any lint on fabrics, especially on the darker ones. A linen or cotton dish towel works better than a terry towel. If at the end of the second laundering process the white towel is still white, I'm fairly confident that there will be no more color running from that fabric.

If the towel does not remain white, the fabric is washed again and again until all the excess dye is gone and the towel does stay white. A clean white towel is used for each laundering cycle.

After all of the fabrics have been individually washed, all of those fabrics to be used together in a given quiltmaking project are put in the washer and washed with warm water only (no detergent) on the permanent press cycle. The theory here is that once the quilt is completed, the fabrics will all be washed together. So I wash them together as a final wash before construction. If anything disastrous is going to happen, I want it to happen before, rather than after construction.

Washing fabrics, in addition to removing excess dye, effectively shrinks the fabrics before use so they won't shrink once they are part of the completed quilt. Some fabrics, especially muslin, may require two or more washings before they are totally preshrunk. Washing also removes excess sizing and finishing on the fabrics and makes them easier to work with. Once the fabric is washed, it must be dried, either an electric or a gas dryer will do. Some quiltmakers prefer to dry their fabrics outside on a line.

The next step is to press the fabric. Use a steam iron for this with the controls set for the fiber content of the fabric. Occasionally, a spray of water from a spray bottle (or from the iron if it is so equipped) may be necessary for handling stubborn wrinkles.

At this point, it is a good idea to remove the selvages from the fabric. If you prefer not to remove the selvages for some reason such as preventing raveling, be sure they do not get incorporated into the quilt. Because their weave is much tighter than that of the fabric itself, they can distort the part of the quilt where they are used, and they can be next to impossible to quilt through. Even as part of a seam allowance they cause these problems, so either remove them at this point or carefully avoid using them.

With today's fabrics, it is frequently difficult, if not virtually impossible, to tell the right side from the wrong side of a solid colored fabric. In order to prevent any confusion, before beginning to mark any fabric, put a safety pin on the top of the wrong side of the fabric. If you can't determine which is the right side and which is the wrong side, make an arbitrary decision and then put the safety pin in the top of what you have decided is the wrong side of the fabric. Be sure this pin stays in place until all the marking is completed.

This will insure against any confusion as to which is the right and which is the wrong side of the fabric, or at least keep you consistent with your choice.

A vital detail to keep in mind during the entire process of marking and constructing the quilt is the grain of the fabric. There are actually three grains to keep in mind when working with fabric. The straight grain of the fabric runs parallel to the selvage. The cross grain of the fabric runs perpendicular to the selvage. The true bias grain of the fabric is at a forty-five degree angle to the selvage. Other angles are also on the bias (Fig. 3). When light strikes the surface of the fabric, it is reflected off and you see the color. If the straight grain of a piece of solid colored fabric is placed verically, the color will appear to be "X." If the straight grain of the same piece of fabric is placed horizontally, the color will appear to be "Y."

True, it won't be an immense difference. For instance, it won't appear red in one direction and blue in the other. But, if the fabric is red, it will appear to be two different values of red when placed in the two different directions. Try it yourself. Cut two pieces of the same fabric approximately 4" wide by 8" long. Lay one vertically and one horizontally forming a large inverted "T" (Fig. 4). In the majority of fabrics you will be able to see quite a difference in value between the two pieces. This same problem occurs with print fabrics although it is usually not as obvious with prints as it is with solids.

FIG. 3

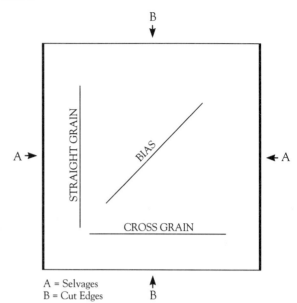

A = Selvages
B = Cut Edges

FIG. 4

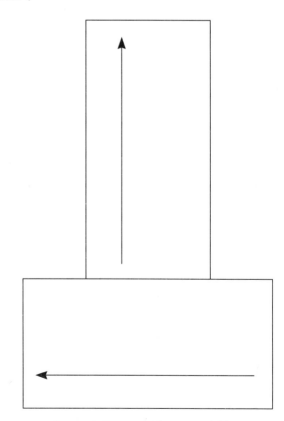

Arrows indicate straight grain of fabric.

In order not to lose track of the grain during the marking, cutting and sewing processes, put a small, single-caretted arrow in the seam allowance of each piece (on the wrong side). The stem of the arrow should be parallel to the straight grain of the fabric and the single caret should point to the top of the fabric which was earlier identified with a safety pin (Fig. 5).

Grain direction can be both a trap and a boon to the quiltmaker. Be haphazard with grain placement and the quilt will have a hit-or-miss quality to it. But you can be consistent or imaginative with grain placement and add another dimension to the quilt.

FIG. 5

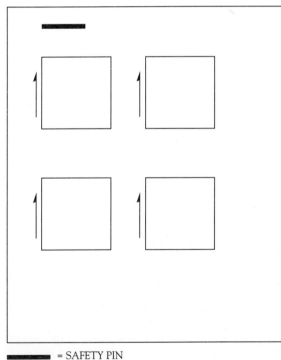

 = SAFETY PIN

Single caretted arrows in seam allowances indicate the straight grain and top of fabric.

PRESSING, PREPARING TOP AND BACK

Pressing. Remember the word. It is an important part of quiltmaking. The word, again, is pressing. This means up and down with the iron. Pressing is not synonymous with ironing. Ironing is putting the iron down on the board and pushing it back and forth in all directions. Ironing is what you do to sheets. (Does anyone still iron sheets?) Pressing is what you do to quilt tops.

Press your top with a steam iron set for the fiber content of the fabric. If your top is a combination of fabrics, set the iron for the lowest setting compatible with the fabric. Use a well-padded board for pressing.

When working with a pieced top, do the final pressing of the top just before the design is marked. Place the top, wrong side up, on the well-padded ironing board. Press all the seam allowances to one side, not open. If you are not certain in which direction to press a given set of seam allowances or an intersection, look at the front of the quilt top at the same time you flip the seam allowances one way then the other on the back. The direction in which the allowances should be pressed is the direction which results in the best looking, most accurate meeting on the front of the quilt top. And if you have heard that you should press the seam allowances under the darker fabric, don't be a slave to this suggestion. If pressing them under the darker fabric results in an inaccurate-looking meet on the top, press them under the lighter fabric and grade the darker seam allowance back (Fig. 6). Check over the back of your quilt top and trim back (grade) any darker color seam allowances that are lying behind a lighter color fabric.

Because of all the seams involved in a pieced top and the likely chance of burning your fingers with the tip of the iron if you try to hold the seam allowances in place while you press, try this approach. Place the area you're ready to press on the ironing board wrong side up. In the very center of the area, turn the seam allowances in the direction you want them to lie and stick a straight pin down through the seam allowances and into the well-padded board. Continue manipulating the seam allowances in the direction you want them to lie, working from the center of the area outward, and securing them in place with straight pins until the entire area is pinned. To press, hold the iron in one hand, pull one pin out with the other hand, starting at one edge of the pinned area, and place the iron down on the fabric where the pin was removed. Hit the steam button, press, and then lift the iron up. Do not move the iron while it is resting on the fabric.

FIG. 6

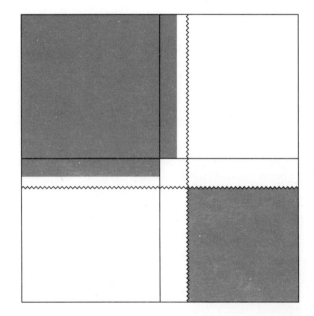

Graded Seam Allowances seen from the wrong side.

Continue in this fashion until all the pins have been removed and the entire area is pressed, and then move to the next area. Move the project and start pinning where you left off and work outward from there until the project is completely pressed. Remember, all pins should be standing straight up during this process.

This may seem at first reading to be a lot of extra work, but it only takes a few minutes to turn the seam allowances and secure them with pins. Once this is done, the pressing goes faster than it would if you tried to turn the seam allowances with one hand and press with the other. Also, you're in little danger of pressing your finger tips with this method. Once the entire top has been pressed from the wrong side, turn it over and re-press it from the right side, being sure that your first pressing has not forced inaccurate meets any place on the face of the top. Remember, press (up and down with the iron), don't iron (pushing the iron around on the surface).

When working with an appliqued top, do the final pressing of the top before the design is marked. Again, press wrong side up on a well-padded board. Use a steam iron at the proper setting. This is a good time to remove any background fabrics that lie behind applique pieces if you wish to do this. It does add to the difficulty of quilting the piece to have this extra layer of fabric so you may want to remove it (Fig. 7). Press the appliqued top from the wrong side, lifting the iron up and down and utilizing the steam feature. The applique top may be re-pressed from the right side if desired. However, many quiltmakers prefer not to do this as they feel it smashes down the applique too much. This is a matter of personal taste – re-press from the top or not, depending on your personal preference. If the appliqued top has been made up of blocks set together or sashed together, these areas are pressed according to the directions for pressing pieced work.

FIG. 7

BACK VIEW
A = Line of applique stitches
B = Cut edge where background has been removed
C = Back of applique piece showing through

FIG. 8

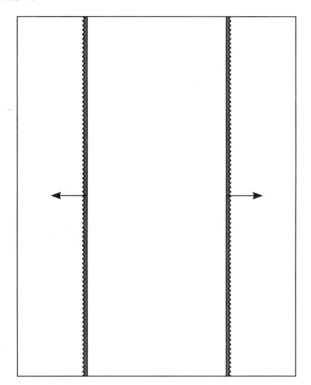

FIG. 9

When working on a whole cloth top, do a final pressing of the top before the design is marked. Press wrong side up on a well-padded board. Use a steam iron at the proper heat setting. If the top has been pieced to make it large enough for the project, it is recommended that a single seam not be placed down the center of the front. It is better to have two seams, evenly spaced on the front. When piecing this, the preferable method is to use a whole width of fabric down the center, with partial widths on either side of it to obtain the desired overall width. This leads to longer wear for the top because any seam stress is distributed between the two seams instead of being placed on a single seam. Also, two evenly spaced seams are less distracting to the design than a single seam down the center. If the whole-cloth top has been pieced, be sure to press the seam allowances to one side and not open. These seam allowances should preferably be pressed toward the outside edges of the quilt, rather than toward the center (Fig. 8).

In addition to pressing the quilt top, the backing must also be pressed. If the backing has been pieced to make it large enough, it is recommended, as with the whole-cloth top, that a single seam not be placed down the center of the back. It is better to have two seams, evenly spaced on the back (Fig. 9).

The reasons for doing this are the same as for seaming the whole-cloth top. When piecing the backing, it is recommended that the piecing be done vertically with vertical lengths of fabric. Having the grain on the backing run vertically places it in the same direction as a large portion of the grains on the quilt top. This should lead to longer wear. Aesthetically, a horizontally-seamed backing chops up the back of the quilt and is less pleasing (Fig. 10). If the backing has a more elaborate treatment, the chosen construction method should be accurately handled and suitably pressed.

Pressing the backing involves simple steam pressing of the fabric. Press wrong side up on a well-padded board. Press any seam allowances to one side and not open. These seam allowances should be pressed toward the outside edges of the quilt. Re-press the backing from the right side.

To reiterate: when doing any pressing for quiltmaking, it's important that the pressing be done on a well-padded board using a steam iron set for the proper heat. Do not iron by pushing the iron around as this can stretch and distort the work. Always press by lifting the iron up and down. That's pressing!

FIG. 10

MARKING TOOLS

The tools you choose to use for marking the quilting design on your quilt top should be chosen with the same care you've given the rest of your planning. This is no time to be casual. The marking tool should be easy to use and it should make a fine line which is visible while you're working and undetectable or removable when the project is completed. The tool should cause no damage to the project in either its use or its removal.

The first choice of a marking method is one that puts no mark of any kind at any time on the quilt top. Clearly this is seldom possible, although for marking straight lines, my choice is masking tape. When you do mark directly on the quilt top, select a tool that will result in a very fine, light line. For light colored fabrics, use a mechanical pencil with a 0.5 mm lead in a 3H or 4H hardness. For dark colored fabrics, try an artist/student silver colored pencil kept well sharpened. On those rare occasions when neither of these tools is visible on a given fabric, use an artist/student yellow colored pencil. I also use the mechanical pencil and the silver pencil when doing any marking for piecing and for applique. But, as with all tools, I use them with caution.

Don't use any tool that would leave a permanent mark such as a ball-point pen or a transfer pencil. These are tools to be avoided at all times and in all cases.

I am very leery about any marker whose chemical properties I can't identify. I am afraid of possible reactions between the fabrics and the properties of the tool over a long period of time, even if the markings themselves are no longer visible. Fade-out pens, double-ended removable pens, washout pens and washout pencils fall into this grouping.

However, many quilters are pleased with the washout pens. But over the past few years

I have seen so many disasters with them that I would not recommend their use. In practice, they make a very wide line and it is difficult to get a straight line of stitches along this wide mark. But the real problems of the washout pen turn up during the removal process. In some cases, the marks are very difficult to remove, requiring much washing and a good deal of time. Sometimes the marks turn dark and seem permanent. Some marks wash out of the quilt top but sink into the batting and spread horizontally in the batting layer, and show through the top. Others wash out of the top and then sink through the batting layer to appear on the back of the quilt. I have seen the marks removed from the quilt top and then reappear again! I don't want to solve this mystery, but merely to avoid it.

The washable pencils also present problems in that they make a wide line unless constantly sharpened. And, as with the pens, marks sometimes wash out of the top, sink through the batting layer and appear on the back of the quilt.

All of these problems lead me to avoid using the washout pens and pencils and to not recommend their use.

Other types of markers may be more or less successful depending on the project, the design to be undertaken and the types and colors of the fabrics.

As implied, once the marking tool has been chosen, it must be used with care. Always test the chosen marking tool on the fabric. The testing should determine the ease of tool use, visibility of line, and removability of marks. Transfer the design to the quilt. Be sure to observe any grain indicators if these are provided with the design. If marking before assembling the textile sandwich, use the marking tool carefully, working on a hard, flat surface that is light colored. If you work on a dark colored surface, you tend to mark too heavily and darkly. If the only suitable marking surface is dark colored, cover it with white paper before beginning to mark. Shelf paper or typing paper work well. An artists' light box is a good surface to use when transferring a design. It is a virtual necessity when you choose to transfer a design by tracing it rather than using a template or stencil. If you don't have a light box, you can rig one by supporting a piece of glass over a light source.

Keep a clean eraser handy while you are marking your design. An eraser made of plastic (synthetic rubber) seems to work fairly well. There are also special quilter's erasers available. Clean the eraser before using it by rubbing it on white paper. If you must erase, erase with the straight grain of the fabric to avoid stretching and to keep the top clean.

Of the methods employed or the tools used to mark the quilting design, some are used before the textile sandwich is assembled while others are used after the textile sandwich is together. Following is a list of most tools quilters have been known to use for marking tops. The list provides information about each tool, evaluates its effectiveness, and indicates whether the marking is done before assembly (ba) or after assembly (aa).

Hard lead pencils (ba)

The pencil should be at least a #3, and even harder lead may be used. This tool should be kept very sharp. It produces thin, light lines that are easy to see close up for quilting and if used with a light hand, hard to detect after quilting. They may sometimes be removed by washing and some quiltmakers choose to remove them by lightly erasing them. The type of hard pencil that's easiest to use is a fine point (0.5 mm) mechanical pencil filled with a hard lead.

Soft lead pencils (ba)

This tool results in a line that is easy to see while quilting. Because the lead is soft, it is difficult to keep a sharp point unless the lead is used with a mechanical pencil; that still doesn't keep it as sharp as most quiltmakers like. Unfortunately, after quilting, the line remains easy to see and detracts from the quilt. Also, the soft lead tends to smudge, and the graphite is picked up by, and carried on, the thread as you quilt resulting in dirty quilting stitches. Sometimes this marking can be removed, with difficulty, by washing.

Dressmaker's marking pencils (ba)

These pencils are usually available in three colors: white, pink, and blue. They are easy to use but nearly impossible to keep sharp. Marks done with them can usually be brushed off after quilting but they do tend to brush off early and need replacing during the quilting process.

Artists'/Students' colored pencils (ba)

These are easy to use and a relatively sharp point can be kept. They are available in a wide variety of colors that makes them visible on almost any color or print of fabric. When choosing these pencils, be sure that the type chosen does not have a heavy grease content.

Draftsman's pencil (ba)

This is an easy marking tool which can be filled with hard lead and sharpened to a very fine point. The results and use are the same as outlined above for the hard lead pencil.

Water soluble pens (ba)

(Also called "washout" or "spit pens.") This tool is easy to use, but makes quite a wide line. It can easily be seen while quilting. However, much caution must be exercised in its use. First of all, it is possible to have it disappear if the weather is very humid. But, the biggest problem is in its removal. It is supposed to come out easily, but this is not always the case. It must be used with extreme care, with directions followed exactly.

Washout pencils (ba)

These are easy to use but must be kept very sharp to avoid making a wide line. Their line is easily seen while quilting, but there can be problems with removal.

Fade-out pens (ba, aa)

This tool is easy to use and its lines are easy to see while you're quilting. The marks from this pen fade out within a certain number of hours so a project can be marked before assembly only if it is a small project.

Double-ended removable pens (ba)

They are easy to use and the marks are easy to see while quilting. You use one end of the pen to mark with and the other end of the pen to remove the marks.

Soapstone pencils (ba)

This tool can be sharpened to a very fine point and it is easy to use. It can be easily seen while quilting on a medium to dark color of fabric. It should be able to be removed by brushing.

Chalk (ba, aa)

Some chalk tends to make quite a wide line while other chalks make a fine line. Chalk lines can easily be seen while you are quilting. Usually chalk needs to be constantly re-marked as it brushes off easily.

Soap (ba, aa)

Soap is easy to mark with and to see while quilting. A fine edge can be kept on the soap for a thin line. It can usually be brushed off after quilting and what doesn't brush off can be washed out. Only pure soaps with no perfumes or creams should be used.

Dressmaker's carbon (ba)

This is easy to use and results in a fine line that is easy for you to see while quilting. But it is extraordinarily difficult to remove. (Not recommended.)

Powdered chalk (aa)

Powdered chalk is relatively easy to use with some practice. But it must be done in only one small area at a time and the process of quilting is constantly held up by the marking. It is easy to see and comes in a variety of colors. It's important to be sure the color(s) chosen can be removed from the fabric.

Masking tape (aa)

Tape is easy to use and, obviously, easy to see while quilting. You quilt right along the side of the tape, and it just peels off. Masking tape comes in a wide variety of widths from ¼" up. It can only be used for straight lines and must not be left on the quilt top for any length of time as it can leave a sticky and/or colored residue on the quilt. Also, if there is any bearding problem with the project being quilted, masking tape tends to aggravate it.

Tailor's chalk (ba)

This type of chalk is easy to use and a fine edge can be kept on it. It is easily seen while you're quilting and can be brushed off. It does, though, have a tendency to brush off early and to require re-marking.

Iron-on transfer pencils (ba)

These are relatively easy to use and the marks are easily seen, but for all practical purposes, they are permanent marks. Avoid this method.

Ball-point pens – (ba)
The pen is easy to use, makes a fine line and is easy to see. However, nearly all ballpoint pens make permanent marks. Avoid this method.

Ribbon, Bias tape, Seam tape (aa)
These items are used the same way masking tape is used but instead of being stuck to the quilt top, they are pinned or basted in place. This does take some practice to master.

Needle pressure (aa)
On a relatively tautly stretched quilt, pressure is exerted on the design lines, around a template or with a stencil with the eye of a needle. The pressure leaves a depressed area on the quilt top and the quilter stitches along this line. Only a small area can be marked at a time as the pressure line does not remain visible for a long period of time.

Bowling pencils (ba)
These are easy to use and leave an easily visible, if somewhat wide, line for quilting, especially on darker fabrics. But the tool has a high wax content and is extremely difficult (if not impossible) to remove. Avoid this method.

Pressure sensitive designs (aa)
These designs peel off a backing and are pressed into place on the quilt top. The design is quilted around and then is removed from the quilt top and repositioned to begin again. These designs can be reused until they will no longer adhere to the quilt top. They should not be left in place for too long a period of time.

The Eye
This technique of marking (or nonmarking) is when you gauge where you will quilt by eye without any marks or device to guide your quilting. On freehand designs or in the ditch this can be a good method of working. But if any quilting line must parallel another one or parallel a seam line, your eye must be extremely accurate or the lines which should be parallel will tend to wander.

Remember, don't use any tool that would leave a permanent mark such as a ball-point pen or a transfer pencil. These are tools to be avoided at all times and in all cases for the reasons stated above. Remember that the marking tool should be easy to use, should make a fine line, should be visible while working, should be undetectable (or removable) when the project is completed, and should cause no damage to the project in its use or removal. The one absolutely inviolate rule for using a marking tool is: *Mark Lightly!*

BATTING AND BACKING

When choosing a batting to use in your quilt, keep certain considerations in mind. First of all, as with anything else, the batting type should be suitable to the top design and to the planned quilting design. The batting should also be compatible with the fabrics.

The batting should provide a certain ease in the quilting and workability; in other words, it should needle well. You certainly don't want to fight every stitch you put in the quilt. Here again, a practice piece is invaluable. Using the fabrics of your quilt top, construct a small textile sandwich using a piece of the batting you are thinking of using in the quilt. Quilt on this textile sandwich and you'll soon know if all the elements in combination lead to a workable quilting situation.

Keep in mind that the thickness of the batt will affect the ease of quilting, the size of the stitches and the overall finished look of the project.

Obviously, the thicker the batt, the more difficult it will be to quilt through. If a very thick batt is desired, for whatever reason, you might want to consider tying the quilt instead of quilting it. It simply isn't worth the effort to quilt a very thick batt because much of the subtle effect of the quilting will be lost due to the thickness of the batt. The physical difficulty of quilting through a thick batt is considerable.

One subject that is a cause for concern is the intervals between rows of quilting or quilting motifs. In the past, quilters had to quilt quite heavily on a project that used a cotton batt to prevent any slippage of the batt and to cut down on the lumping during laundering. With the advent of synthetic batts, quilters felt free to do less quilting, leaving larger intervals between rows of quilting or quilting motifs. The amazing thing is that the recommended intervals between rows of quilting or quilting motifs on a synthetic batt vary widely from source to source. I have read recommendations for intervals on a synthetic batt as small as one inch and as large as twelve inches. But, after experimenting, I have come to the conclusion that the empty space between rows of quilting or quilting motifs on a synthetic batt should be no larger than four inches. Obviously, a quilt with a synthetic batt can be quilted more heavily than this, but as a rule, you should leave no more than a four-inch space open (without quilting). Also, four inches may be too large an interval to leave unquilted from a design point of view even though it may be acceptable from a technical point of view. The maximum empty space between rows or motifs on a cotton batt should be no larger than one inch. But remember, these recommendations are a result of experimentation and are not hard and fast.

Ultimately, a choice has to be made on the type of batting to be used. The most traditional batting is the cotton batt. As mentioned, a cotton batt needs to be heavily quilted to prevent slippage. A cotton batt tends to separate and lump during the laundering process. Many individuals still prefer to use a cotton batt because they like the look of the finished project. The only time I would consider using a cotton batt would be in combination with an old cotton top. However, even then I might decide against it because of the difficulty in quilting. A synthetic batt needles more easily than a cotton batt.

The synthetic batt is my choice in almost all circumstances because of the ease in quilting and because I like the look of the finished project. I prefer to use a thin synthetic batt, as I feel this provides the best showcase for the quilting. But the use of a synthetic batt has its own built-in set of problems, the foremost one being bearding. While not all synthetic batts beard, a large percentage of them do. Bearding is fiber migration and this means that the batting tends to filter through the top of the quilt. This does not mean that little wisps of batting come through the top when the needle is pulled through and it does not mean pilling that is the result of abrasion during the use of the quilt. Both of these problems can happen with a synthetic batt, but they are not as severe a problem as bearding. The bearding appears evenly all over the top of the quilt, making the top appear to be in need of a shave. This bearding is more apparent if there are dark colors in the quilt top, but it is still present, if not as noticeable, when light colors are used.

Blends instead of cottons in the top fabrics seem to add to the bearding problems, but bearding can still happen if only cotton fabrics are employed. It is possible to underline the top with lightweight fabric to help cut down on the bearding, but that means there will be four, instead of three, layers to quilt. It is also possible to "shave" the completed quilt by clipping off the bearding. This will help on a temporary basis but the fiber migration will continue after a time. Also, cleaning up the bearding is a long and tedious process. In addition to bearding, some synthetic batts have hard spots in them while others are not totally even and flat but have hills and valleys. Now, quality control means that any given brand of batting should give the same degree of performance each time you use it. But these days it is difficult to rely on quality control; a given brand can differ in performance from purchase to purchase.

Another type of batting currently available is a blend of cotton and polyester. Most quilters wash this batting before use and this makes it easier to quilt. If you haven't tried this blend batting, you could try a practice piece and see

if it meets your needs.

Wool batting is, of course, warm. It can be successfully used with cotton tops. The wool batt requires approximately the same amount of quilting as a cotton batt does. Wool batts, if not available locally, are available through mail order.

Silk batting is extremely easy to quilt and it drapes very nicely for use in garments. The silk batting that is available most generally comes in cones which can be difficult to separate and it is also difficult to lay it out on the backing to achieve an even layer of batting. Unfortunately, I have seen silk batting beard when used with cotton top and backing fabrics and when used with silk top and backing.

Polyester fleece is easy to quilt and gives a nice look to the finished project. It is only available up to 45" wide, but it works very well in small quilted pieces.

Finally, it is possible to quilt a piece without any filler/batting at all. This type of quilt would provide little warmth, but would still be effective in warmer climates or for summer quilts in colder climates. A quilt with no filler would be very easy to quilt and very small quilting stitches would be possible.

The type of quilt batting you choose will depend on all the above factors and may well vary from piece to piece. There is no single batting that is the best for use in all circumstances. You need to look at each project thoughtfully and then choose the best batting for the circumstances involved. But for quilts and wallhangings, in general, choose synthetic batts.

The "look" of the finished bed quilt will depend on many of the above factors plus the amount of quilting in the design combined with the thickness of the batt. A flat quilt tends to look more traditional. This can be accomplished by using a relatively thin batt and a good deal of quilting. A less flat quilt tends to look more modern. This is achieved by using a somewhat thicker batt and relatively less quilting.

It is a good idea to "rest" the batt before using it. Open the batt and allow it to remain open and flat for about twenty-four hours. This will allow any wrinkles caused by packaging and storing to relax and flatten. Good quality batts will usually "relax" within twenty-four hours. Should the batting still be terribly distorted after the twenty-four hours, you can try to flatten it and put it into shape. If this doesn't work, you may want to consider discarding this batt (or using its flat areas for small projects) and replacing it rather than using it in the quilt and hoping the distortions will be able to be quilted out. Sometimes they will quilt out and sometimes they won't, and there is too much work and time involved in the quilting to take a chance.

All of the various types of batting seem to have their own built-in problems. Quiltmakers have to decide which problems they would prefer to live with and this will determine what batting should be chosen. The batting that the individual finds easiest to quilt and that yields the best looking finished project will wind up as the batting of choice.

Once the batting has been selected, the backing and the batting need to be prepared. Be sure to allow extra fabric in the backing for "take up" during quilting. There tends to be more "take up" in quilting done in the hands than in quilting done in a frame or a hoop. The actual amount of "take up" for a given project depends on the individual quiltmaker and the style of quilting employed. You can determine your average personal "take up" by doing a practice piece. Baste a 15" x 15" textile sandwich with the top marked with any quilting design. After it is completely quilted, measure the finished project. If it is finished 14½" x 14½" after quilting, you know that your personal "take up" is approximately ½" for every 15" of quilting. Remember, though, that

this is just a guideline because the amount of "take up" can be affected by the amount of quilting in a given area or by the materials you are using. Finally, when all is considered, it is still possible for the personal "take up" amount to vary somewhat from time to time for any individual.

Cutting the fabric requires sharp concentration and an even sharper pair of scissors. When cutting the fabric, the backing fabric should be cut larger than the top and the batting. You should also, of course, consider the type of quilt it is and the type of finishing you have in mind for it. In general, the backing should be at least 3" larger on each side keeping in mind the overall size of the project. Cut the backing fabric 3" larger than the quilt top on each side for any project up to and including a crib quilt. The larger the overall size of the project, the more extra backing that should be allowed on each side. For a king size quilt, cut the backing fabric about 6" larger on each side.

When cutting the batting, it should be cut larger than the top but smaller than the backing. In general, the batting should be at least 2" larger on each side of the quilt top. The larger the overall size of the project, the more extra batting that should be allowed on each side. Again, for a king-size quilt, cut the batting about 4" larger on each side.

On occasion it may be necessary to piece a batt to get the desired size. One way of piecing a batt is to lay the edges of the two pieces right next to each other on a hard, flat surface, butting them together. Use a large stitch and sturdy thread and overcast the edges together (Fig. 11). Care needs to be taken to be sure that the two pieces of the batting do not overlap as this will cause a lumpy area, a sort of ridge, in the completed quilt. Care also needs to be taken to be sure that the two pieces of batting do not separate as this will cause a thin area, a kind of ditch, in the

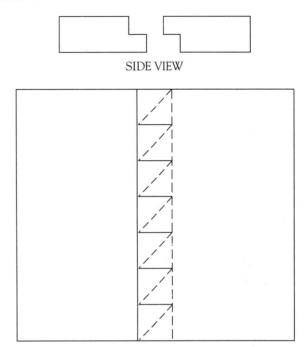

FIG. 12

SIDE VIEW

TOP VIEW

completed quilt. Another effective way of piecing a batt is to cut a small step or ledge from the side of one piece of batting. An inverted step or ledge is cut from the side of the other piece of batting. The two pieces of batting are brought together on a hard, flat surface and the little steps or ledges are fitted together (Fig. 12). Use a large stitch and sturdy thread to whip the two pieces together. Both of these methods work for piecing batts. The latter method is slightly more difficult to do but there is less chance of a problem with it in the long run and it is the method preferred. Of course, don't piece a batting unless it's absolutely necessary.

FIG. 11

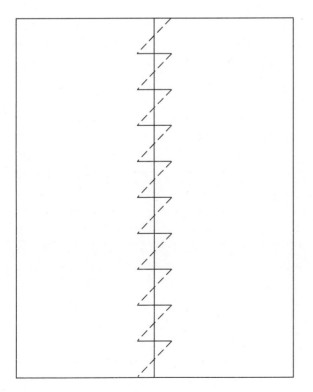

The reason for allowing extra batting and backing when preparing the textile sandwich is to guard against any shifting of the work during the quilting process. You will sometimes see quilts with small triangular wedges added to the backing along one side near the top and along the other side near the bottom because the work has shifted (Fig. 13). This can certainly detract from the overall look of the finished project. It is just easier to plan ahead for problems of this type and allow the extra fabric. You can always cut it off if you don't need it. Having the extra fabric around the edges also allows additional options in finishing the edges of the project.

Allow additional extra fabric around all sides of the quilt top itself, as well as the batting and backing, if the project is to be incorporated into another item, say a pillow or a tote bag. This extra amount to be allowed can be determined by the intended use of the project, but at least 1" should be added to the seam allowances on the outside edges of the top to be certain there is enough fabric to join the quilted item into the future project. Remember that it is always easier to cut off excess fabric than it is to add it.

FIG. 13

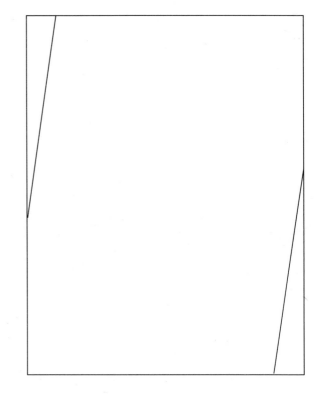

ASSEMBLING THE TEXTILE SANDWICH

Before beginning to assemble the textile sandwich, the first task is to clean the wrong side of the quilt top. Be sure that all the seam allowances have been graded where a dark fabric has been pressed behind a light fabric. Also, be sure that no seam allowances are wider than ¼". Remove any pet hairs. Remove all schnibbles. "Schnibbles" is a term I use for any loose threads or any fraying, semi-loose threads from seam allowances. If these schnibbles are not removed and the top is placed on white batting, they will almost certainly show through and haunt you. This is especially true if, for instance, a thread of navy is lying behind a piece of white fabric. If you miss a schnibble and only discover it after the quilting is complete, it can sometimes be removed. Use a #13 steel crochet hook to carefully part the fibers of the quilt top. Slip the crochet hook between the parted fibers, hook onto the schnibble with the hook and gently pull it out. Rub the area where the fibers were parted with your finger tip or the blunt end of the crochet hook or the eye end of a needle to return the fibers to their original position. It's easier to remove schnibbles in the first place, before quilting.

For the back of an appliqued top, be sure you've carefully cut away, wherever possible, any background material which lies behind the applique pieces if you've decided on this procedure. Again, remove any pet hair and schnibbles.

For the back of an embroidered quilt top, once again be sure to remove any foreign particles. Be certain there are no tails of embroidery floss hanging loose. Be certain, also, that the embroidery floss has not "traveled" for long distances where it will show through the top. If there are long "traveling" threads between embroidery stitches, clip them, remove the excess thread and knot them off close to the stitches. If you prefer not to knot, secure threads carefully at the site of the stitches.

For the back of a whole-cloth quilt top, you know what to do: get rid of pet hairs, schnibbles, or other extraneous matter.

The assembling of the textile sandwich may be done on a basting frame, a large table, or a floor depending on what is available to you and how you feel comfortable working. The first step in the assembly of the textile sandwich is the layering, and the first layer that is put down is the backing. It is placed wrong side up, right side down. If the piece is square, be sure that the straight grain of the backing is lying in the same direction in which the majority of the straight grain of the top will be placed, that is, vertically. The backing should be smooth, flat, and totally wrinkle-free. If working on a table or floor, you can secure the backing to the surface with masking tape. One more time: check to be sure there is no extraneous matter on the backing. If working on basting frames, secure the backing to the frames themselves, depending on which type of basting frame you are using.

The second layer to be put down is the batting. This should be smooth, flat, and totally wrinkle-free. Be sure the batting has been allowed to "rest" as discussed in "Batting and Backing." Move the batting with care to avoid tearing it and to avoid pulling it so much that some areas become stretched thin. Now what do we do? Check to be sure there is no extraneous matter on the batting. The batting should be exactly centered on the backing.

The final layer to be put down is the quilt top. This should be smooth, flat, and totally wrinkle-free. It should be exactly centered on

FIG. 14

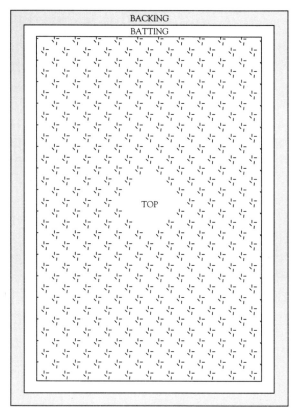

the other layers (Fig. 14).

The next step in the assembly of the textile sandwich is pinning together the three layers. Use long, thin pins with large round heads. Pin through all three layers, inserting pins parallel to the outside edges of the textile sandwich. Twelve pins can be used to secure the outer edges of the layers. Insert pins in numerical order (Fig. 15). These twelve pins should be sufficient to hold the project during the basting process. However, if you would be more comfortable with additional pins, put more in. Note that no pins are used in the corners. The pins should be removed as soon as you baste up to them. If you baste past a pin, you could baste bubbles or pleats in around the edges of the project. Keep a careful count as you remove the pins to be sure that you take twelve pins out (or however many you put in). This is important because you don't want any of the pins to slip into the quilt to reappear painfully later.

The layering and pinning of the textile sandwich in preparation for basting is an important step and should not be done carelessly or in a rush. All of the layers should be smooth, flat, and totally wrinkle-free. The quilt top should be carefully centered on the other layers. Remember to count the pins carefully as you remove them.

FIG. 15

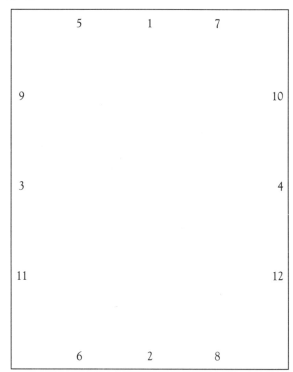

BASTING THE TEXTILE SANDWICH

Basting thread is an important part of the quiltmaker's choices. Commercial cotton basting thread is cheap, easy to use and white. This is what I use and what I recommend. Of course, any cotton thread can be used for basting, but it should be a light colored cotton thread, preferably white. If dark colored cotton thread is used for basting, it can leave little dots of color when the basting is removed. This is especially true if the basting is left in for a long period of time or if you live in a damp climate. It's not worth taking a chance, so stick to basting thread or white cotton thread for basting.

Embroidery (crewel) needles are handy to use for the basting process. Embroidery needles are long with long, large eyes making them easy to thread and easy to slip through the layers during the basting process.

Baste the three layers of the textile sandwich together. There should be sufficient basting to hold the layers together securely without shifting. Try using a sunburst effect layout (Fig. 16) for the basting as it allows any excess fabric in any of the layers to be worked out toward the open edges during the quilting process without being trapped by the basting lines. The trapping of any excess can lead to pleats and bubbles being quilted in, especially on the back of the quilt. This trapping of excess fabric during the quilting process can easily happen if the basting is done on a grid of crossing lines (Fig. 17). Also, the sunburst effect easily allows for additional lines of basting to be added if the quiltmaker feels they are necessary.

FIG. 16

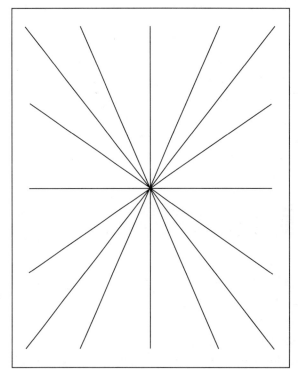

FIG. 17

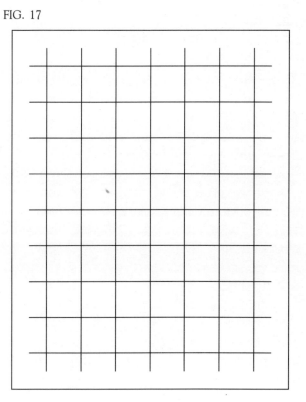

For any project over 24" x 24" in size, use a full complement of basting lines (Fig. 18). Using an embroidery needle or long darner will facilitate the basting. Use a piece of basting thread about 12" longer than the length of the line to be basted. Start using the center of the thread and begin at the center of the line to be basted. Baste toward #1. As you approach the pin, remove it, baste to the edge, do two backstitches and clip the basting thread leaving about a 1" tail. Re-thread the needle at the center of the thread and, again beginning at the center of the quilt, baste toward #2. As you approach the pin, remove it, baste to the edge, do two backstitches and clip thread, leaving about a 1" tail. Repeat this procedure for basting lines #3 and #4, #5 and #6, #7 and #8, #9 and #10, #11 and #12, #13 and #14, #15 and #16, basting in numerical order. Using this basting process with a full length of thread, half of it to baste in one direction and half in the other, eliminates the necessity of having any basting knots in the center of the quilt. If there are basting knots in the center of the quilt, they can cause distortion, something you want to avoid.

Basting line #17 is a series of eight short basting lines running half the length of one side or end of the textile sandwich. Begin each of the basting lines at the center of one side (or one end) with a knot and end it at the corner with two backstitches and a 1" tail.

If additional lines of basting are desirable, or seem necessary, add them, beginning each line at the indicated place on the diagram (Fig. 19). Start each of these basting lines with a backstitch at the place indicated, baste to the edge, do two backstitches and clip thread leaving about a 1" tail.

Some smaller projects may not require as much basting as full-size projects. For these small projects (up to about 24" x 24"), use the basting layout diagram that is designated for smaller projects (Fig. 20). Follow the same

FIG. 18

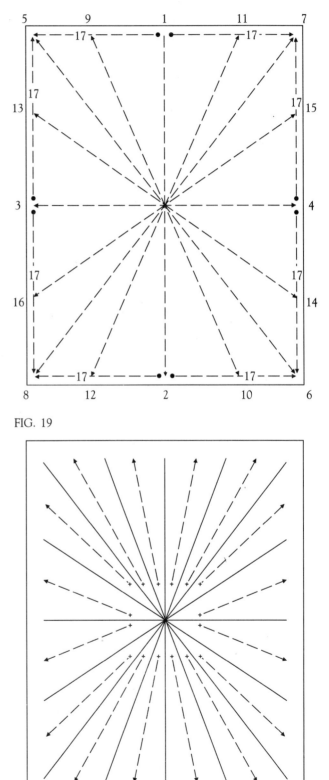
FIG. 19

+ = Beginning point for each additional basting line.

FIG. 20

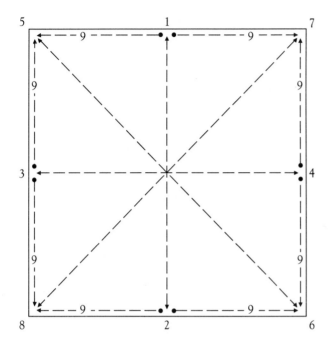

procedure as outlined above by starting the basting with the center of a long length of thread at the center of the piece you are basting.

The size of the stitches used for basting varies from quilter to quilter. Obviously, the basting stitches don't need to be as small as quilting stitches, but neither should they be too big. Big basting stitches can allow for too much shifting among the layers of the textile sandwich. As a rule, basting stitches about ⅜" to ½" long are effective in holding the layers together without undue shifting.

Whenever possible, baste toward yourself. If this isn't possible, baste parallel with yourself. Avoid basting away from yourself as this direction is more difficult to control and could cause distortion. Don't baste directly on top of a marked quilting line since basting stitching might interfere with your quilting and result in a less than smoothly quilted line. Move the line of basting slightly to one side or to the other of the marked quilting line.

Remember that during the assembly of the textile sandwich twelve pins (or however many) were put in. Be certain that all twelve pins (or however many) are removed during the basting process.

When the basting is completed, check the back of the textile sandwich to be sure it is still smooth and wrinkle-free. If there are any distortions of the backing such as pleats or bubbles be sure to remove the basting stitches that are causing these distortions and re-baste. This may seem like a lot of work but there is no point in starting to quilt a project with distortions already in it. While it may be possible to quilt around them and work them out the open edges, it is far more likely that the distortion will be permanently quilted in.

If the backing has been firmly secured to the table or to the floor with masking tape, use a spoon to facilitate the basting. Place the tip of the bowl of the spoon at the place on the quilt where you want the needle to exit. (The handle should be pointing up, perpendicular to the quilt, and the inside of the bowl should be facing toward where your needle will emerge.) Push the needle through the textile sandwich. The needle will "bounce" off the surface you're working on, and when it hits the spoon, it will slip out of the top of the textile sandwich and slip up the bowl of the spoon, making it easy for you to pull it through without stabbing yourself. A plastic spoon can be used for this, but a stainless steel spoon is better since it is sturdier and easier to use than plastic. Don't use a silver spoon as the bowl does become scratched. You will find that you can build up a smooth basting rhythm using the spoon technique and the basting task can be painlessly speeded up.

If you have access to basting frames, you will find the basting easier to do. It is easier to handle the textile sandwich on the frames and it is easier to do the basting. It is also possible to place the textile sandwich in the basting frames and pin baste (instead of thread baste) the entire project using small nonrusting safety pins. The operative word here is nonrusting.

If, at any time during the quilting process, the basting stitches begin to distort the work, clip the offending basting stitch. Don't remove the line of basting, just clip it where it is causing the problem.

The basting process is crucial to the quilting. A well-basted project will speed up the quilting and allow you to do your best quilting without the extra problems of shifting layers, bubbling, and pleating. Take the time to do a thorough basting job and you will find it worth your while.

FIG. 21

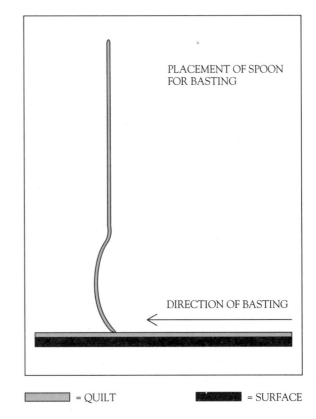

PLACEMENT OF SPOON FOR BASTING

DIRECTION OF BASTING

= QUILT   = SURFACE

WORKING METHODS

When quilting your project, you have the choice of working with it on a frame, in a hoop, or in your hands. You can also work on the full project all at once or only a block or section of the project at a time.

Working on a frame can give your work a flatter, smoother finished appearance. Of course, a frame takes up a lot of space. Unless you have a studio set aside for your quilting or unless your living room, family room or bedroom is large enough to accommodate a frame with ease, the space factor is very important. You don't want to be constantly bumping into a quilting frame, or to have family members tripping over it, especially while you're quilting. A frame can also be awkward for some people to use since you have not much option as to the direction in which to quilt. Because the quilt is secure in the frame, you must quilt in whatever direction the quilting design takes you. And, more importantly, you must maintain a consistency in your quilting stitch no matter which direction you are quilting. You may find yourself stuck in your chair at the frame trying to quilt toward yourself, away from yourself, to the left and to the right. It helps some if you are ambidextrous (or if your arms are long enough!), and your quilting frame is a rolling one and narrow enough, to quilt from either side of the frame. But quilting on the frame does seem to result in a quilt with straighter edges and squarer corners than one quilted in other ways.

Working in your hands can give a puffier finished appearance to the work. However, the entire project (especially large projects) can be difficult to control and handle. The finished product can be less than smooth. This method doesn't require a great deal of space, although the bulk of the quilt will have to be supported on your lap, on a snack tray, or on a footstool.

It can be a very warm undertaking during the summer months and it can be a cumbersome way of working at any time. However, you will be able to quilt in the direction most comfortable for you. You also will be able to put the project in a large tote bag and carry it anywhere you want to do your quilting.

Working in a hoop can give a flatter, smoother finished appearance to the work. You can quilt in whichever direction is comfortable for you and a hoop takes up little space and is also very portable. When placing the project in a hoop, be sure that the bottom of the project (the backing) is smooth in the hoop and that the tautness of the backing and of the top in the hoop is equal. The tautness should be evenly distributed, and for this reason, I prefer a round to an oval hoop. I find it is easier to get the project consistently taut in a round hoop than in an oval one. Experiment to see whether the round hoop or the oval hoop works better for you.

Rest the project on a table to take the weight off the portion of the quilt in the hoop and this will also help prevent stretching. Add fabric strips around the outside edges of the quilt so the border areas can be quilted with the same tension as the rest of the quilt. Remember that these added fabric strips should be of the same thickness as the textile sandwich itself. I prefer to baste terry cloth towels of the appropriate thickness (they can be folded to get the desired thickness) to the outside edges of the project so that the final borders can be quilted with the same degree of tension as was used for the central portion of the project.

One or both pieces of the hoop may be wrapped with muslin strips if desired. This wrapping can help prevent slippage so the textile sandwich will be maintained at a better tension in the hoop for a longer period of time. Also, wrapping the hoop helps prevent any snagging of the quilt and this can be important depending on the types of fabric you are using.

Do not leave the quilt in the hoop between quilting sessions. Remove the hoop when you reach the end of your quilting for the day and replace it when you begin quilting.

Quilting a block or a section at a time is Sectional Quilting, although it is also called by many other names. This method has each block or section quilted before the parts are all assembled into the quilt. Often this method is recommended to beginning quilters so they won't be faced with such a massive project as quilting a complete quilt at once. However, I have found that only really accomplished, consistent quilters can handle this method with a large degree of success. Because of the "take up" in quilting, each block can end up varying widely in size, and it can be very difficult to assemble the quilted blocks into a complete quilt with any degree of accuracy. If the quilt is composed of 12" blocks, one block could quilt up to 12", another to 11¾", another to 11⅞", and another to 11¹⁵/₁₆". Assembling these various sized quilted units then becomes a nightmare. When assembling the blocks, the corners won't match and it will be nearly impossible to get the project to lie flat. This problem is compounded in the making of a sampler quilt where the amount of quilting may vary from block-to-block, or section-to-section, thus making the problem of "take up" more complicated. Unless you are a very consistent quilter, and the amount of quilting in each block or section you are doing is nearly identical, the sectional method is not recommended. Keep in mind that Sectional Quilting is not so much a method of quilting (the quilting is still done either in a hoop, in a small frame, or in your hands), as it is an assembly technique.

I have found that I do my best quilting when stitching from northeast to southwest (I am right-handed). Frame quilting does not always allow me to do this. On the other hand, I find the quilting stitch much easier to control and the finished product more pleasing when the project is held taut during the quilting process. Quilting in my hands does not provide the tautness I find necessary to do my best work.

Therefore, in most cases, I prefer to work with a hoop. This allows me to work on the entire project, holding it at the degree of tautness I require. It also allows me to quilt in the direction which results in my best quilting stitches, provides portability, and does not consume space.

Each of the above working methods has its own advantages and disadvantages. You may want to experiment with each method to find the one that works best for you – the one that gives you the best quilted finished product and that you enjoy the most. Remember to be flexible and keep an open mind on the subject of working methods. There may be times when one method works well for you and other times when a different method works well on a different project. But if this is your first time trying to quilt a complete project, try it in a hoop.

THREAD AND NEEDLES

It should go without saying that you use a good quality thread for quilting. Using a poor quality thread that will snarl, fray, fuzz, wear thin, and break is not worth the hassle. Quilting should be an enjoyable process and the use of good quality thread can add to the process while poor quality thread can lead to aggravation – and even spectacular additions to your vocabulary.

There are a variety of threads available today, and many of them have a place in quiltmaking. For the most part, it is easier to quilt with quilting thread than with other threads. Quilting thread comes in a fairly wide range of colors, but you may find it necessary to go to a sewing thread for quilting if your choice of color is not one of those available. Quilting thread is available in cotton and cotton covered polyester. Some cotton quilting threads are wiry while others are limp. Both of them work well. I prefer to quilt with cotton quilting thread of either type. I like the way it quilts and I like the look it gives the completed project.

Sewing thread can be used for quilting but this would be my choice only if I couldn't get the color I wanted in quilting thread. But sewing thread is my choice for all piecing and applique work. Sewing thread is available in both cotton and polyester as well as cotton covered polyester. While the best advice is to use the same type of thread, either cotton or polyester, as is in your fabrics, many quiltmakers use polyester thread or cotton covered polyester thread on cotton fabric for piecing and applique. The main reason for this is the ready availability of polyester sewing thread in an incredibly wide range of colors. Perhaps somewhere down the road it will be proven that the combination of polyester thread and cotton fabrics does not hold up. But in the meantime,

it is a fairly common combination.

Silk thread can be used for quilting, but it does tend to fray quite easily. However, it is a lovely thread to quilt with and comes in a good variety of color choices. If silk thread is your choice for quilting a special project, try using very short lengths of the silk thread in the needle.

The old needleworker's aid, beeswax, can be used to coat and strengthen the thread used for quilting and it will sometimes help control the tangling of the thread. At other times, however, the use of beeswax seems to encourage the batting to stick to it as you quilt and to be pulled through the top of the quilt in little wisps. Experiment to see if your quilting in any given project is helped or hindered by the use of beeswax.

All of the technical considerations aside, a very important choice the quilter must make is the color of the thread that will be used to quilt the project. The color of the thread used can give the illusion of affecting the quality and the size of the quilting stitches even though it is not actually doing so. Stitches made in thread that contrasts in color with the fabric will appear larger than stitches made in thread that matches the color of the fabric. The sharper the contrast between the color of the thread and the color of the fabric, the larger the stitches will appear to be.

For inexperienced quilters, it is usually a good idea to match the color of the thread to the color of the fabric being quilted. More experienced quilters will find fewer problems in using a thread color that contrasts with the fabric color. Occasionally, people will find that they don't like to use many colors in quilting thread; they don't like the presence of many colors on the back of the quilt. If you think this will be a problem for you, consider using a print on the back of the quilt. If a print is used, remember it shouldn't shadow through the top. Again, do a practice piece. This will help you be certain that the thread will work well, both aesthetically and technically, with your chosen fabrics and batting.

Once you have decided on the thread you are going to use for quilting, you must determine how to use it. Consider the following pointers on the use of the thread when quilting:

1) Use a single thread for quilting. Double threads are not necessarily stronger than single threads as they tend to wear against each other thus reducing the strength. Double threads can also give a messy look to the work.

2) Use an 18" length of thread – maximum. Any longer length of thread will tend to fray during the quilting process. Also, every time the thread is pulled through the quilt, there is a certain amount of wear on the thread. So a thread longer than 18" will wear and not be as strong as it should. By the same token, it is better not to use a single length of thread for quilting many short lines with lots of beginnings and endings. Instead, use many new short lengths of thread for these short lines of quilting. Remember that while the recommended length of thread for quilting is 18" maximum, shorter lengths can always be used. The single exception to the 18" maximum length will be discussed when we look at the quilting of circles.

3) Cut the thread at an angle rather than straight across. This will make it easier to insert thread into the needle. Knot the end of the thread that you cut from the spool. This can help cut down on thread twisting. It doesn't always help, but it helps often enough to make it worth acquiring the habit. Use a small, round, clean knot. Experiment with the quilting thread, fabric, and batting practice piece to determine the best size knot for each particular piece.

4) If the thread begins to twist on itself and tangle while you're quilting a piece in a hoop or in your hands, turn the work upside down and let the needle dangle while the thread untwists. Or twist the needle in the opposite direction in your hand. If you are working on a frame (or sometimes in a hoop), move the needle down the thread until it is lying flat on the quilt top and straighten and untwist the thread with your fingers. Then return the needle to the proper position on the thread and continue quilting.

5) Keep the loose end of the thread relatively close to the top of the quilt while you are working. Move the needle down the "tail" of the thread every few stitches. This will eliminate excess wear in any one spot of the thread by the needle. This is called "riding the needle" and refers to the way in which the needle rides on the thread closer and closer to the thread's loose tail end as you work.

6) As a special caution, never stick your needle into the thread wound on a spool as a resting spot. This will break and weaken the thread on the spool. Keep your needles stuck in a needle book or needle case and not in the spool (or in the arm of the sofa).

Since thread is one of the vital ingredients of your quilt, take the time to decide which is the best thread to use on any given project, and the color that will most enhance it. Above all, never settle for inferior quality thread.

Just as quiltmakers have a variety of fabrics, battings, and threads from which to choose, so they also have a variety of needles available to them. The obvious choice of a needle for a quilter is a quilting needle. These short needles are also called "betweens." The theory is that these short needles will give you smaller quilting stitches because your fingers will be closer to the work, giving you better control for more even stitches.

"Sharps" are needles that are longer than quilting needles. Sharps are also a perfectly acceptable type of needle to use for quilting. Some quiltmakers find sharps more comfortable to quilt with than quilting needles. This may be especially true for quiltmakers who have long fingers and who may feel they have better control with the longer needles.

As well as having your choice of the type of needle and the length of the needle with which to work, you also have your choice of diameters to use. The lower the number of the needle, the bigger the needle. For instance, a #10 needle is finer than a #6 needle whether you're working with quilting needles or sharps. The finer the needle is, the more easily it will slip through the fabric while you are quilting.

Both quilting needles and sharps are useful for piecing, applique, and quilting. As with anything else, experiment with the types of needles to determine which type is the most comfortable for you. In addition, experiment with the size of needles available to find the size needle with which you most like to work. Beginners can start working with a #8 needle. After gaining some experience and confidence with a #8, it is a good idea to switch to a finer needle such as a #10.

Replace your needle if it becomes dull or too bent, if it gets a burr at the point, or if the eye area is rough. Needles are not expensive so there's no point in using a needle that is difficult to handle or won't give you good stitches. Polyester fibers tend to dull needles more quickly than cotton fibers so your needle may need to be replaced more often when working with these fibers. Some quilters prefer to use a slightly bent needle but care should be taken that it doesn't become so bent that it's difficult to control. If you have strong fingers you may find that you bend a fine needle quickly. In this case, use a slightly heavier needle.

Probably one of the greatest annoyances in any type of hand sewing is threading needles. Many people hate to thread them so much that they tend to use a thread that is much too long. Remember that 18" is the maximum length of thread you should use. If you are experiencing difficulty threading a needle, turn the needle around and try threading the needle through the eye from the other side. Many needles have a groove on one side which is slightly longer and larger to facilitate threading. When threading a needle, hold it over white paper or white fabric. This tends to make the needle's eye more visible and easier to thread. Also consider using a needle threader to make threading easier. This can be especially important, even vital, when using very fine needles.

To take some of the aggravation out of threading needles, try multiple threadings. Thread an entire package of needles onto your spool of quilting thread. This will take a few minutes but will get the threading task out of the way for a while. When you need more thread, pull the 18" of thread through all the needles, leaving a final needle on the thread, then clip the thread leaving the rest of the needles still threaded onto the spool.

As with any tool or material for quiltmaking, be sure you are using good quality needles and take care of them. Avoid jamming them into hard surfaces; store them in a needle book or needle case. Never leave a needle anchored in your work for that could be the one time when the needle you're using might rust. This isn't supposed to happen, but it has happened, and it's better to guard against it than to be faced with fixing the problem.

Once you find a needle type and size that suits you well, stock up on them. You will find you can use them for most of the projects you'll be working on. For those occasions when they won't suit, reasonable substitutes are readily available.

WORKING WITH THE QUILTING DESIGN

Design factors can govern, to some extent, the quality of the quilting stitches. Each single element of the quilting design is important to the overall quilting design. Before making a final decision on the quilting, study the elements of your chosen design to be certain you can handle all of the elements in relation to the fabrics and batting you are using.

Quilting on the straight of grain is the most difficult direction in which to stitch. It is difficult to handle the needle and to penetrate the textile sandwich. Visually, the quilting stitches on the straight of grain are not terribly effective because the quilting thread tends to sink between the fibers of the fabric. Straight of grain quilting stitches do not seem to integrate as well with the quilt top but tend to distract from it.

Fig. 23

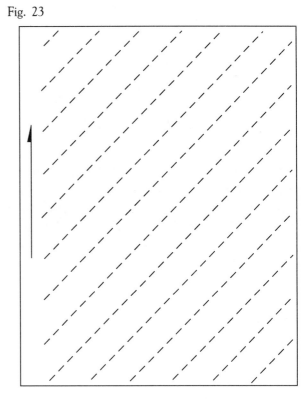

Fig. 22

Fig. 24

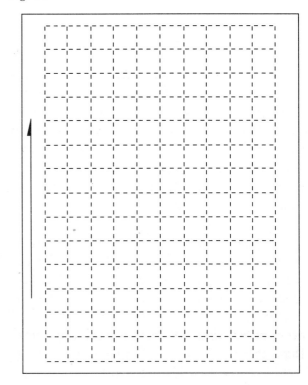

42

Quilting on the cross grain of the fabric is somewhat less difficult than quilting on the straight of grain. Visually, these stitches are somewhat more effective than straight grain stitches. But again, they do not seem to integrate thoroughly with the top design (Fig. 22).

Quilting on the bias of the fabric is very easy to do. The needle will be easy to handle and the textile sandwich can be penetrated with ease. Visually, quilting stitches on the bias are very effective. They can be seen while at the same time they seem to complement any top design or quilting design (Fig. 23). Of course, there has to be a catch here, and there is – quilting on the bias provides the highest likelihood of having the quilting line wobble. The bias of the fabric is not as stable as the straight and cross grains so unless the fabric is held securely, the individual stitches on the bias may not be as straight as you would like and the entire line may wobble. Also, when quilting on the bias, great care must be exercised to avoid stretching the quilt. It is easy to have this happen when you are quilting in your hands, but it can also happen when quilting on a hoop or a frame.

If the quilter desires to use background quilting to enhance the top design and the rest of the quilting design, use straight quilting lines on the bias rather than on the straight or cross grains. If a grid or cross-hatching is desired, follow the same recommendation. Instead of a grid of crossing straight and cross grain quilting lines (Fig. 24), use a grid of crossing bias quilting lines (Fig. 25). You will find the bias grid easier to quilt and the resultant quilting lines will integrate well with the rest of the quilting design and with the top design. If there is no other quilting design, you will find a bias grid more effective when used alone than a straight or cross grid. The bias grid you choose can have lines crossing each other at 90° (Fig. 25) or at a more acute angle (Fig. 26).

Fig. 25

Fig. 26

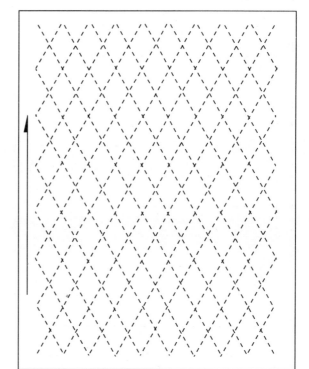

If a grid of crossing lines is used, be certain that it is evenly maintained across the quilt. If a grid is uneven, the quilt will give the illusion of tilting.

Many effective quilting designs used in the main area of the quilt top or in the border areas also include curves. Curved quilting lines are graceful, effective, and add to the overall look of the quilt, but caution should be exercised in their use. Care should be taken not to straighten-out areas of the curve, but to keep the entire curve smooth. Most often, you will straighten-out the outside bend of the curve, especially where the outside curve is on the straight or cross grains of the fabric (Fig. 27). If you allow these curved lines to straighten-out, you will not get a graceful look to the quilting, but rather a choppy appearance that will not be effective and will not enhance the quilt.

Fig. 27

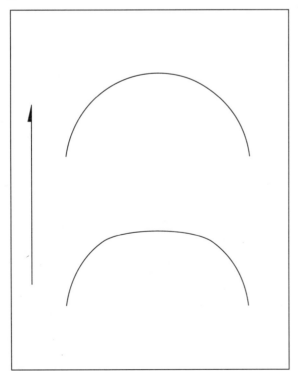

When quilting curves, take care not to lose stitches on the back of the quilt while quilting from bias to straight grain or from bias to cross grain. The same care needs to be taken when quilting from straight grain to bias and from cross grain to bias (Fig. 28). It is not unusual for the stitches in these areas to slip off the needle leaving empty spans on the back of the quilt (Fig. 29). In each case, only a couple stitches are involved. You can actually hear them drop off the needle. Listen carefully while you are quilting in these areas and if you hear them drop off, back the needle out and redo the stitch(es) before continuing. It may also help if you do one stitch at a time when quilting in these areas.

When quilting multiple parallel curved lines, the same problems exist as discussed above for quilting single curved lines – straightening-out on the curves and dropping stitches on the back. Additionally, you will have to exercise care to keep the lines totally parallel (Fig. 30). It is very distracting to look at parallel lines that aren't really parallel. First of all, be sure your pattern lines are parallel before transferring them to the quilt top. Then stitch carefully on the lines. But, don't depend totally on your drawn design to keep the lines parallel. Use your eye as an additional guide and keep checking the sweep of the previous curve to be sure the current curve is following the same sweep.

Take care not to have too much relief (puff) between multiple parallel curved lines (or multiple parallel straight lines). This extra relief can be distracting visually and it adds to the amount of "take up" in the quilting. If there is too much relief between lines of quilting, you could end up with pleats or bubbles stitched in. Also be sure that the amount of relief between the multiple lines is consistent from one area to the next.

When quilting parallel lines, it is important to keep them parallel as discussed above.

Fig. 28

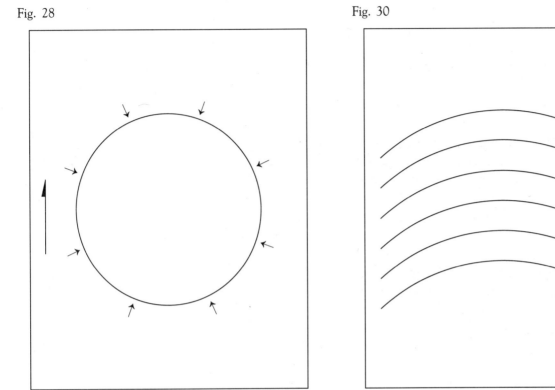

Fig. 30

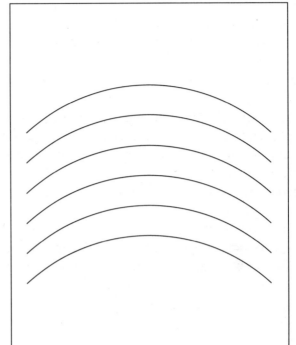

Fig. 29

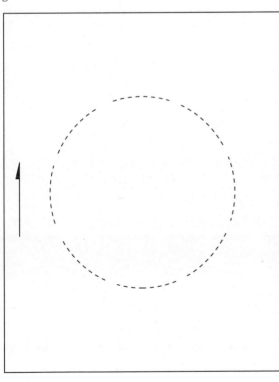

But it's also important to quilt all parallel lines in the same direction. For instance, if there are parallel lines running diagonally from the top right to the bottom left of the work, start each line of quilting at the top right and end it at the bottom left (Fig. 31). In other words, quilt each line from the northeast to the southwest. If you switch directions when quilting parallel lines, the quilt can be distorted. The quilt top and back will tend to ripple or pull between the parallel rows of quilting (Fig. 32). Therefore, don't quilt the first line from the northeast to the southwest, the second line from the southwest to the northeast, and so on. If you do, you're inviting trouble. This same caution holds true whether you are quilting straight parallel lines or curved parallel lines.

Fig. 32

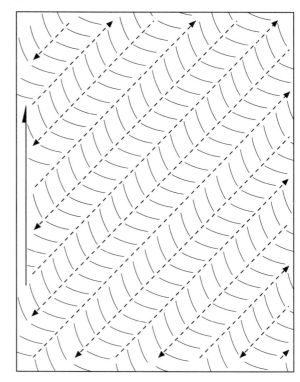

Fig. 31

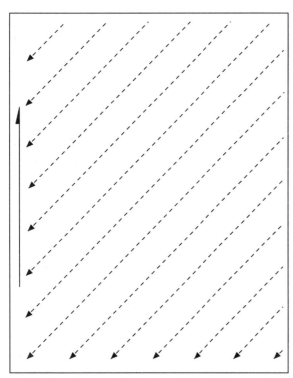

Fig. 33

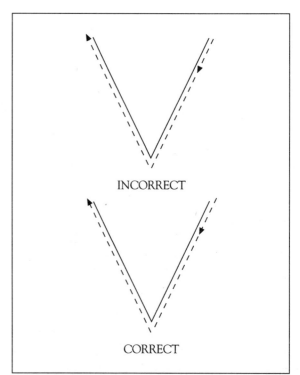

INCORRECT

CORRECT

In addition to quilting straight lines or curves, you'll frequently quilt around corners and points, such as quilting around the perimeter of a square or the points (inside and outside) of a heart shape. I use the term "around" deliberately as that's what happens most of the time. The corners or points are quilted "around" and the result is that the sharp corner or point is rounded and lost. To avoid this, gauge your quilting stitch length to allow your needle to come up at a corner or point, instead of going down. The final stitch at a corner or point tends to curve rather than to lay straight, thus giving a rounded instead of a sharp corner or point. It is better if this slightly curved stitch is on the back of the quilt, rather than on the front. Remember, instead of going down with the needle at corners and points, bring the needle up at a corner or point and this will result in their being sharply quilted (Fig. 33).

There are very few quilting designs that do not have lines that cross at some point. Care has to be taken when crossing previously quilted lines. Don't allow pleats or tucks to form on the front or the back of the quilt at the junctures where quilting lines cross. These lines may be crossing at right angles or at angles of other degrees. Quilting in a hoop or frame helps to prevent the formation of bubbles and pleats where the lines cross. If you are quilting in your hands, hold the area taut when quilting across previously quilted lines. But don't pull the section so tight that it becomes stretched; just hold it taut. If you find that you are getting pleats or bubbles at these intersections when quilting in a hoop or frame, use your fingers from below to push the quilt up slightly, resulting in a little extra tension or tautness in the area.

When approaching a previously quilted line from any angle in preparation to crossing it, try to gauge your stitches so that you cross the line with the thread on the back of the quilt. If you cross the previously quilted line so that the thread is on the top of the quilt and lies across a stitch of the previously quilted line, you will have a small "+" or "x" at the intersection (Fig. 34). If this happens with any frequency, it can be visually distracting, but there is no problem if it happens occasionally. It is even more distracting if the color of your quilting thread contrasts with the color of your fabric. Remember, it's a matter of gauging your stitches to avoid this problem.

Fig. 34

Whenever you are quilting, it's important to keep your straight quilting lines straight and your curved quilting lines curved. This applies both to the individual stitches and to the entire line of stitches. Each stitch should be straight and the entire line should be straight (or curved lines should be curved) depending on the pattern (Fig. 35). First, be sure that your pattern has been transferred correctly onto the quilt top and stitch exactly on the pattern lines. If a pencil line has been used, be sure it is a fine line. Obviously, it is much easier to get straight stitches if you are following a fine line than if you are following a wide one. If for some reason you have a fat line, stitch down the dead center of the line or along one side or the other of it. Just taking the needle from one side to another of a fat line can make a line of quilting stitches crooked (Fig. 36). Keep your eye ahead of where you are quilting and this will help you get straighter lines or give a better sweep to curved lines.

Frequently your quilting design will include circles. This is the only instance where it's all right to use an extra long piece of quilting thread. Start with the needle at the center of the long piece of thread and quilt halfway around the circle and end off. Rethread the needle at the center of the long piece of thread, quilt the other half of the circle and end off. This technique results in a quilted circle with two endings and no beginnings (Fig. 37).

However, some people cannot quilt comfortably around a circle in both directions. If this is true for you, start quilting and quilt all around the circle in the same direction, ending and beginning as often as needed, using 18" of thread in the needle each time. I am one of those who has difficulty quilting in two directions in the same circle. I can comfortably quilt above the top of the curve and so I go all around the circle working above the curve. I find that when I quilt below the curve, my

Fig. 35

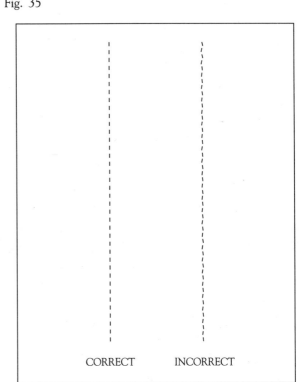

CORRECT   INCORRECT

Fig. 36

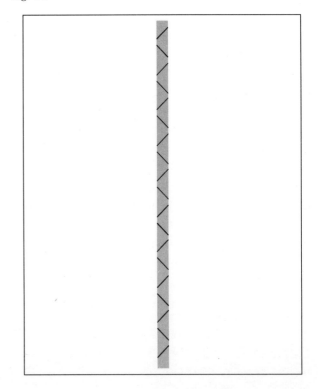

Fig. 37

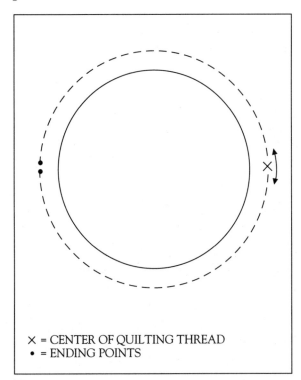

X = CENTER OF QUILTING THREAD
• = ENDING POINTS

Fig. 38

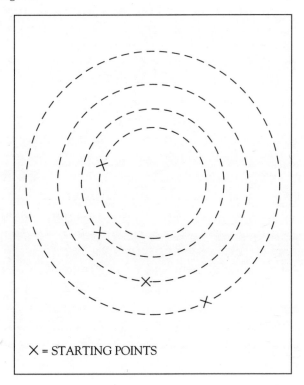

X = STARTING POINTS

circles aren't smoothly curved and my stitches aren't as controlled. Test yourself on this two directional technique and see if it works for you.

When quilting concentric circles, it is a good practice to stagger your starting point on each of the circles (Fig. 38) so that the starting and ending points on the circles do not end up in a row. Begin quilting the center circle at any point on that circle. When you complete the quilting, end off the thread, or travel through the center layer (batting) and begin quilting the second circle at least one needle's length ahead of where the quilting on the center circle began. Continue this practice on each succeeding circle.

All of the factors discussed in this chapter will govern, to some extent, the results you get when quilting. All of them need to be given consideration when planning your quilting design and when doing the actual quilting. Curves should be curved, straight lines should be straight, and corners and points should be sharp. Just thinking ahead and gauging your stitches can make an enormous difference in the effectiveness of the quilting. Keeping in mind all of these factors will help you make better design choices and get the best results from the quilting stitches.

THE QUILTING STITCH

The first concern in executing the quilting stitch is how to begin the line of quilting. There are a variety of ways that quiltmakers start quilting lines, and for that matter, a variety of ways that quiltmakers end them. Some of these starting and ending ways are very good techniques and others don't work as well. It seems best to both start and end the quilting line with double security. This is the method I use myself, it is the method I teach my students, and it is the method I recommend to you.

To start your line of quilting, thread your needle with an 18" length of thread (remember that maximum) and make a small round knot at the end of the thread. Be sure that the knot size is compatible with the top and back fabrics and batting. The knot should be small enough

to pop through the fabrics and large enough to anchor in the batting layer. Determine the point at which you want to start the line of quilting – this is point "A." Locate a point one needle's length ahead of point "A." Ahead means the direction toward which you will be quilting – this is point "B." Insert the point of the needle in the back of the quilt at point "B" and bring the needle on a slant through the batting and out the top of the quilt at point "A." Slowly pull the thread through until the knot rests on the back of the quilt at point "B." Wrap the thread around your forefinger and tug sharply. Don't pull with a steady pressure, but give a sharp tug. Pulling with a steady pressure can tear or distort the backing fabric, so be sure to use a sharp tug. The knot will pop through the backing and into the batting. You will hear the knot pop through. As soon as the knot pops through the backing and into the batting, release all pressure on the thread. You want the knot to stay just where it popped through near point "B" and not be pulled through the batting toward point "A" (Fig. 39).

If you are having problems popping the knot through the backing fabric or the knot breaks off, the knot is probably too large. Try again with a smaller one. If the knot pops all the way through and out the top, the knot is probably too small. Try again with a slightly larger knot. The purpose of popping the starting knot through the back of the quilt instead of through the top is to cut down by fifty percent the possibility of tearing the quilt top. Admittedly, it would be extremely rare to tear fabric by popping a knot. It would be more likely to slightly pull one of the fibers, but you certainly wouldn't want to take a chance. You would definitely hope that popping a starting knot would not cause a tear, but if it did, it is

Fig. 39

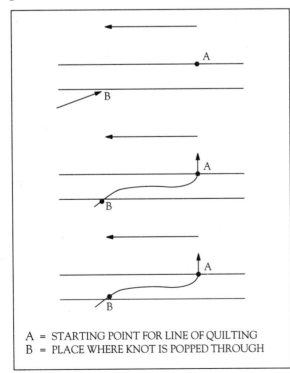

A = STARTING POINT FOR LINE OF QUILTING
B = PLACE WHERE KNOT IS POPPED THROUGH

better to have to fix the tear or pull on the back of the quilt than on the top.

Knot in place, start quilting from point "A" toward point "B." In these first few stitches you will penetrate the thread that lies buried in the batting between the starting point "A" and where the knot is secured in the batting near point "B" (Fig. 40). This starting technique has double security because of the knot and because the thread buried in the batting layer has been anchored by the quilting stitches. If the color of the quilting thread is a good deal darker than the top fabric, be sure the thread is buried quite deeply in the batting.

The quilting stitch itself is a small, even, running stitch that goes through all three layers of the textile sandwich. Make every effort to get every stitch and space on the front and the back to be the same length (Fig. 41). This is not something that happens magically when you pick up the needle to begin quilting. It's something that requires much practice. Keep working on getting the stitches even. Once you have the stitches and spaces quite even, you can begin to reduce the stitches and spaces in size in order to get those small stitches you yearn for.

But until you get the stitches even, don't worry about their being extremely tiny. In fact, if at the moment you are getting very tiny stitches on top, along with large spaces on top and uneven stitches and spaces on the back, I would advise you to lengthen your quilting stitch on top to match it to the space until they are even and then practice getting them smaller. It is much easier to achieve evenness in this way than in any other.

It may sound strange to hear someone advise longer quilting stitches, but in the overall pursuit for evenness, this method works well. If you try to get the spaces as tiny as the stitches you will usually end up with a lot of poor stitches that are still not even. Small stitches

Fig. 40

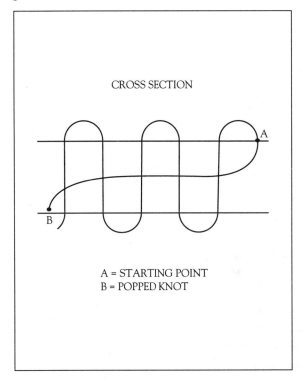

CROSS SECTION

A = STARTING POINT
B = POPPED KNOT

Fig. 41

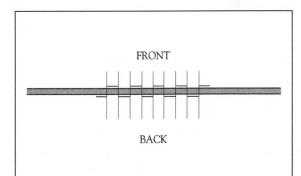

FRONT

BACK

Fig. 42

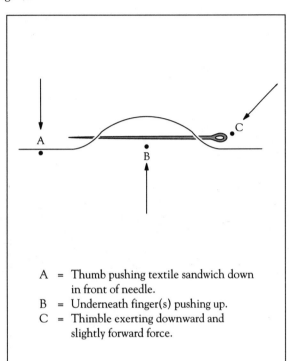

A = Thumb pushing textile sandwich down
in front of needle.
B = Underneath finger(s) pushing up.
C = Thimble exerting downward and
slightly forward force.

are something to be worked toward, but they are not so sacred that everything else must be sacrificed for them.

However, when I talk about making the stitches longer to match the spaces, I am talking about long as a relative term; I do not mean inch-long stitches. Just make them slightly longer to get them into proportion with the spaces. Then try to reduce both stitches and spaces at the same time so they are both smaller while still retaining their evenness.

The quilting stitch is executed by inserting the needle straight down into the textile sandwich, going through all three layers and coming out on the back. The needle is not pulled through to the back but is moved forward and immediately tipped sharply upward and through all three layers to the top again. When quilting on a frame or hoop, the easiest way to accomplish the quilting stitch is to situate the point of the needle in the place where you want it to go down, the needle being vertical and perpendicular to the quilt with the point of the needle just touching the quilt top. Place your thimble on the eye end of the needle. Place the side of your thumb on the quilt top where you want the needle to emerge. Push the eye end of the needle flat against the quilt top with your thimble and move the needle very slightly forward. The needle will go through the quilt and will be felt by the finger(s) of the hand that is under the quilt. Use the finger(s) of the underneath hand to force the point end of the needle upwards. What you are doing is creating a flat downward force and a slight forward force on the eye end of the needle, and a downward force on the quilt top with the thumb in front of the needle while at the same time exerting upward force from below on the needle (Fig. 42). This pushes the needle back through the top leaving a small stitch on the back.

More than one stitch may be put on the needle at one time. If you want to put more than one stitch on the needle, lift the eye end of the needle to the vertical position and begin the second stitch as soon as the first stitch is completed as outlined above. Of course, it is sensible to protect the underneath finger(s) in some way while you are executing the stitch.

While quilting in your hands (without a frame or a hoop), hold the needle vertically in the fingers of your top hand and push it straight down through all three layers. Push at least half the needle out through the back of the quilt, removing the fingers of the bottom hand from under the needle point as soon as the needle penetrates the back. Hold the part of the needle on the back of the quilt flat against the back with the middle finger of your underneath hand while the thumb of the underneath hand is curled around the excess fabric and is on top of the quilt, flat over the area where the needle is lying on the back (Fig. 43). Pull the needle back, keeping it parallel with the quilting line and exerting an upward pressure with the needle point until the stitch is the desired size. Push downward with the thumb and middle finger of the underneath hand just in front of the needle point while pushing the needle forward with the top hand and bring the needle back through to the top.

If you wish to put a second or subsequent stitches on the needle before pulling it through, as soon as the first stitch of the series is on the needle, roll your top hand over toward the other side (elbow and all across your body) till the needle is once again vertical and repeat the above detailed process. At first this will feel awkward, but it will result in even stitches on the back and the fingers of your underneath hand will remain blood-free.

The key factor in achieving even quilting stitches is to insert your needle into the textile sandwich at a very sharp angle (Fig. 44A) and not at a shallow angle (Fig. 44B). This is vital when quilting in a frame or a hoop. This will result in a more even stitch on the top and a

Fig. 43

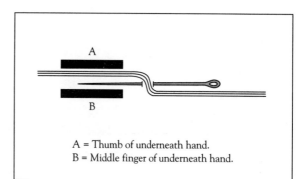

A = Thumb of underneath hand.
B = Middle finger of underneath hand.

Fig. 44A

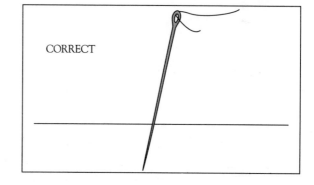

CORRECT

Fig. 44B

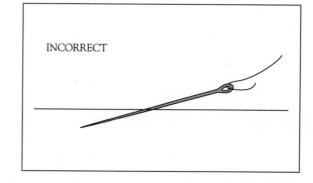

INCORRECT

Fig. 45

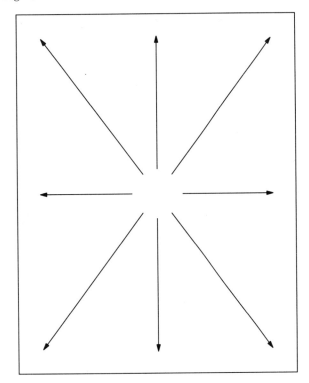

more even stitch on the back. Similarly, bring the needle out at a sharp angle. This again requires practice. When quilting in the hand, the quilt can be raised and lowered with the fingers, easily adjusting to the needle, so that such an acute angle of penetration may not always be necessary. It is still recommended, though, in order to get the most even stitches.

While you are quilting, use a thimble to protect your pushing finger. The correct thimble size is very important. The thimble should not be so loose that it either drops or flies off the finger. It should not be so tight that it affects the circulation or is painful. If your fingers have a tendency to swell, keep two different sized thimbles handy and use the one that fits better at any given time. Deep dimples in the thimble will help control the needle better and thus help to better control the stitches. The needle eye end won't tend to slip off the thimble so readily if the dimples are deep. Be sure not to trap the quilting thread between the eye end of the needle and the thimble as this will cause the thread to wear and fray.

Try several different types of thimbles until you find the kind that is most effective and comfortable for you. Remember, it's better to invest time learning to use a thimble than it is to bleed! In addition to wearing a thimble to protect your pushing finger, it's a good idea to protect your underneath finger also. For this purpose, you can use another thimble of the usual type, or a soft leather thimble, a rubber file finger or one of the commercial finger protectors available. Again, it's a matter of investing the necessary time to learn to use these items effectively. In the long run, it's worth it as you'll be able to avoid callouses, bleeding and sore, pricked fingers.

Whether you are quilting in a frame, on a hoop, or in your hands, start your quilting of a work in the center of the project and work outward toward the edges (Fig. 45). This insures that any extra fullness in the layers of the textile sandwich gets worked toward the outside open edges of the quilt and doesn't get trapped and quilted into the project.

Adjust the length of the quilting stitch to suit the fabrics and batting being used and the type of project being quilted. Loosely woven fabrics seem to require longer stitches since part of each stitch tends to remain sunken in the fibers of the cloth. Slightly larger than usual quilting stitches will compensate for this by allowing for the extra part of the stitch to remain sunken. At the same time, the amount of stitch visible will be approximately the usual size of your stitch. While these stitches may hold the layers together, they do not provide the desired design effect. A heavy batting won't allow for tiny stitches, so work to get even, probably somewhat larger stitches if your batting is relatively heavy.

If the quilting design for a pieced quilt requires quilting across a large number of seam allowances, adjust the length of the other quilting stitches (those that only go through three layers) to match the length of the stitches going across the allowances. It is much easier to make stitches through three layers big enough to match stitches through five layers than it is to make stitches through five layers as small as the stitches you make through three layers. This will result in an even look overall. If the quilting design for an appliqued quilt requires a good deal of quilting on the applique pieces, adjust the length of the other stitches (those that only go through three layers) to match the stitches on the applique piece. This, too, will result in an even look overall to the quilting. Removing (trimming away) the background underneath the applique pieces will result in just three layers to quilt through (See Fig. 7).

Don't commit yourself to pulling the needle through the quilt until you're certain the stitch, or stitches, are correct, that is, until the stitches and spaces are even (Fig. 46). Pull the needle

Fig. 46

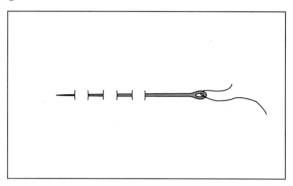

through the work and once the needle is about two inches out from the top of the work, pull the thread only, not the needle, to complete the stitch placement (Fig. 47). The thread can fray more quickly at the eye end of the needle if all the pulling is done with the needle. If for any reason you are experiencing difficulty pulling the needle through the quilt, use a needle puller. Some quilters use small needle-nosed pliers for needle pulling. A circle cut from a balloon is also effective, as is an inch length cut from a wide rubber band. Slip the cut piece of the balloon or rubber band around the needle and then pull. The rubber grips the needle and allows it to be pulled through quite easily. A small piece of masking tape around the point of the needle can also help you pull it through. There are inexpensive commercial needle-pullers available also, as well as various sizes of metal needle-pullers.

If quilting in the hands, quilt toward the holding hand, not parallel to it or in some other direction (Fig. 48). Keep the holding hand still except to raise and lower the textile sandwich to meet the dictates of the needle and the quilting stitch. Don't manipulate the textile sandwich in such a way that you will be forcing extra fullness into the areas between the lines of quilting. If you do, you will find the straight lines you thought you'd quilted won't be straight at all.

The number of stitches you can put on a needle at one time depends on many factors – your quilting experience, the design itself, the fabric and batting, and whether you're quilting in your hands or on a frame or hoop. For each project or for each area of the design, determine the number of stitches that can be put on the needle at one time and still result in even, small stitches on the quilt. Work with as few or as many stitches at a time as you find comfortable for any given project or as works best for any given design.

You will find that even if you take one

Fig. 47

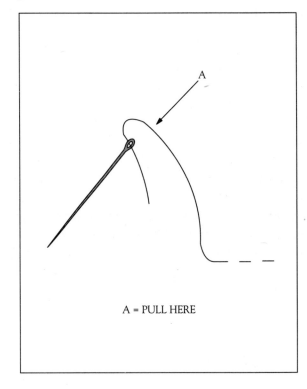

A = PULL HERE

Fig. 48

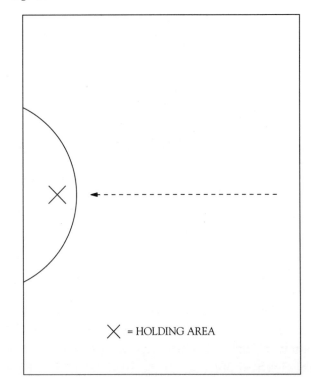

X = HOLDING AREA

stitch at a time, you can develop a good rhythm and quilt quite quickly, so it's an option worth considering. While getting many stitches on the needle at a time seems to speed up the quilting process somewhat, if the resultant stitches are not even, it is not worth the time saved.

If you do put multiple stitches on the needle at a time, the first stitch is the most crucial. It is while gauging the first stitch of a series that it is most difficult to match that stitch and space with those that will come after it on the needle, and those that have already been stitched. Take extra time and care in gauging the size of this first stitch in a series. If you are currently doing a good job of quilting by putting multiple stitches on the needle, continue doing so, and by the same token if you are currently doing a good job of quilting by putting one stitch on the needle, stick with that.

As to the number of stitches to the inch in quilting, I simply don't bother counting them. The number of stitches per inch can be affected by so many variables (fabric and batting among others) that counting stitches is not at all a reliable guide to the overall effectiveness of the quilting. The quilting stitch should be even and small. Tiny stitches for the sake of tininess that sacrifice evenness or detract from the overall quilting design are not the most successful. If you feel you must count stitches, for whatever reason, you can count the stitches showing in an inch on the top of the quilt, or you can count the stitches and add the spaces showing in an inch on the top of the quilt (this would give you the number of stitches per inch on the front and back of the quilt). Whichever way you count, always include the method of counting when stating the number of stitches per inch. For instance, "this quilt has ten stitches to the inch counting top stitches," or "this quilt has twenty stitches to the inch counting top and bottom stitches."

Just remember that while this measures the size of the quilting stitch, it is no indicator at all of its quality.

As you quilt it is important to establish a rhythm to the stitching. Once a rhythm has been established, the quilting stitches will be more even. You will also gain better control of the tension of the stitches. A smooth rhythm will enable you to pick up speed as you work.

In addition to developing a smooth rhythm while quilting, it is necessary to build an even tension into the stitching. The quilting stitches should be tight enough to actively hold together the three layers of the textile sandwich. They should not be pulled so tightly that they form bubbles or gathers that would distort the quilt. However, they should not merely lie loosely on the quilt. Remember that one of the jobs of the quilting stitch is to hold the layers of the quilt together; adjust the tension of the stitch so it does just that, neither more nor less.

When you complete quilting in one area or around one motif of the design and still have a supply of thread in your needle, it is not always necessary to end off the line of stitching. Slip the needle into the center layer of the quilt and "travel" to the next area or motif to be quilted. "Travel" no more than two needle's lengths. If the next area or motif is farther than two needle's lengths away, end off the stitching and restart in the new area. Remember that this "traveling" is done in the batting layer of the quilt and never on the top or the back of the quilt. If the thread color you are using for quilting is considerably darker than the fabric color, travel deeply in the batting or avoid traveling altogether.

During the quilting process, if any of the basting stitches begin to get tight and distort the work, clip the offending basting thread(s). Don't remove the line of basting. Leave it in place to continue holding the layers of the textile sandwich so they won't shift. Just clip them, don't remove them.

If you think it is necessary to remove the quilting stitches for any reason, use the eye end of the needle to pick them out. Don't use the point of the needle as it is so sharp that you may pick up one of the threads of the fabric as well as the quilting stitch and harm the quilt top. For the same reason, don't use the point of the pin. Don't use the point of a scissors, either, as it would be too easy to clip the quilt top.

Don't leave the needle stuck in your work for too long a period of time, and as far as I'm concerned, two minutes is too long. The needle could work its way into the center of the quilt and lay there waiting to stab you at a future time. And, even though needles aren't supposed to rust, if they're left attached to your work for a long period of time and you're in a damp climate, you're courting trouble. When you stop quilting, for whatever reason, remove the needle from the thread and put the needle in a safe place. When you're ready to resume quilting, re-thread the needle.

Whenever you begin a quilting session, it takes a bit of time to re-establish your optimum quilting rhythm and stitch. This amount of time can be anywhere from ten or fifteen minutes to a half hour depending on the individual. If possible, don't quilt in too small segments of time. If you quilt in small segments, you will just get to a good stitch when you have to stop. As a consequence, your work for the segment will have all of these "establishing" stitches in it and few really good stitches of the best quality. Use these small segments of time to work on piecing and applique. Schedule quilting sessions for a period when a solid block of time is available, at least an hour.

If you are quilting on a very special piece, spend the first ten minutes (or so) of your quilting session working on a practice piece such as a pillow top or potholder. I quilt two needles full of thread (a total of 36") on a practice piece before I begin quilting on a special project. Try to get your practice piece to be as close as possible to the main project in terms of fabric weight, type of batting, and backing fabric. If you don't have anything you can use for a practice piece, buy what is often called "cheater cloth," cloth with a printed design you can quilt around. Get enough to make a square 45" x 45". Back it with the proper batting and backing and use it for your practice piece. The completed practice piece makes an impressive everyday kitchen tablecloth – not everyone has hand-quilted kitchen tablecloths! Only you and your family will know that all your rough starting stitches are in the piece.

The quilting line is ended when you reach the end of a pattern design motif or when you are running low on thread. Be sure to have about 3" of thread left in the needle so you can comfortably end the line of quilting. The line of quilting will end with a knot. Working with the thread that emerges from the top of the quilt, place the tip of your left index finger on the quilt top above and to the left of your last stitch. Arrange the thread so that it encircles the finger and you will have formed a soft loop (Fig. 49).

Hold this loop in place with your left index finger, place the point of the needle under the loop and pull the needle through the loop, continuing to hold the loop in place with your finger (Fig. 50). Hold the loop in place and continue pulling the needle, allowing the loop to get smaller. As the loop gets smaller, a capital "Q" will be formed. Do not remove your index finger from the loop as it will be holding the "Q" in place on the quilt top.

Place the point of the needle over the bottom right arc of the curve of the "Q," under the tail of the "Q," and over the bottom left arc of the curve of the "Q" (Fig. 51). Do not pull the needle through. With your right

Fig. 49

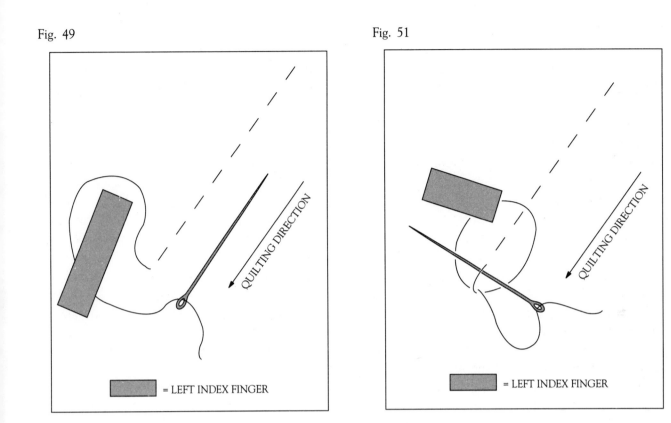

= LEFT INDEX FINGER

Fig. 51

QUILTING DIRECTION

= LEFT INDEX FINGER

Fig. 50

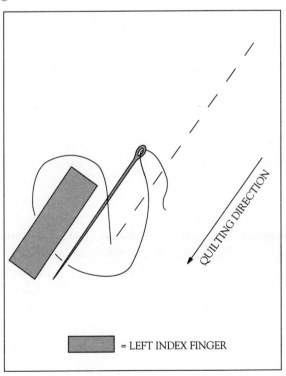

QUILTING DIRECTION

= LEFT INDEX FINGER

Fig. 52

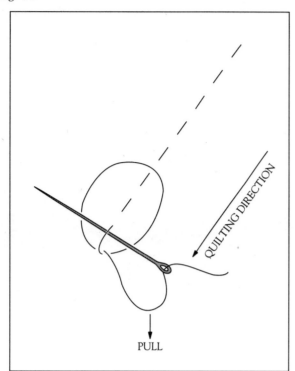

hand, hold the needle flat against the place where the thread emerged from the last quilting stitch. With your left hand, pull the loop tightly into place around the needle, forming the knot (Fig. 52). *Back* the needle out and you'll have a small round knot (Fig. 53). This knot is too small for a secure hold and you will need a double knot.

Repeat the entire knotting process, only this time don't hold the needle flat against the quilt top to tighten the knot. Rather, hold the needle against the first knot to insure the second knot falling directly on top of the first knot, forming a secure double knot (Fig. 54). On those occasions when you are working with a fine thread for quilting, it may be necessary to make a triple knot. This is done in the same way the double knot is done, plus one.

Fig. 53

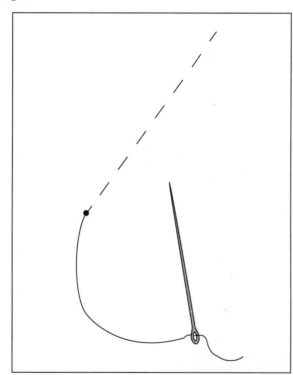

Fig. 54

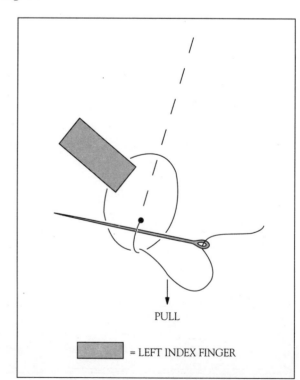

Now that you have formed the knot, it's necessary to bury it. Put some tension on the knotted thread by pulling it back in the direction from which you have been quilting. Put the point of the needle down into the center layer (not through to the back) in exactly the same spot where it emerged from the quilt top (Fig. 55). Push the needle directly ahead in the center layer as far as you can and bring the point of the needle out through the quilt top a full needle's length ahead. Do not pull the needle out of the quilt top entirely; pull it only far enough so the needle has some play in it and bend it over backwards. With your thimble against the point of the needle, push the needle (with the eye leading) another full needle's length through the batting layer. Push the eye end of the needle out through the top of the quilt. Pull the needle and thread out and unthread the needle. Place the needle under the knot to keep twists from forming and pull the thread till the knot is resting on the quilt top and remove the needle. Put some tension on the thread and a bubble will form in front of the knot. With the point of the needle, pick up a little stitch in this bubble but don't catch the quilting thread in this little stitch. Wrap the thread around your forefinger and tug sharply and the knot will pop through the top and into the batting. As mentioned before, don't pull steadily, but give a sharp tug. Clip the thread at the point where it emerges from the quilt top (Fig. 56). Popping the knot into the batting layer by placing tension between the end of the thread and the bubble in front of the knot will help avoid damaging your quilt top.

Fig. 55

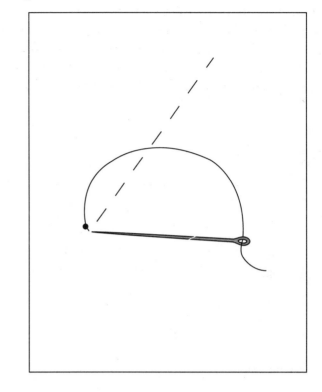

Fig. 56

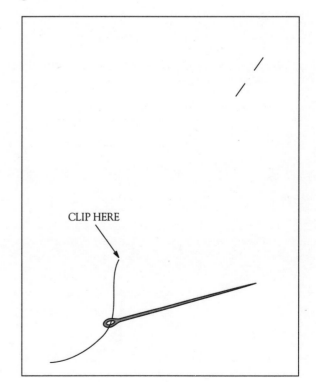

CLIP HERE

If you are running low on thread when quilting a continuous line and have to knot off somewhere midway along that line, the exact spot where the knot was popped through the top in order to bury it becomes the new starting point to continue that line of quilting (Fig. 57).

Fig. 57

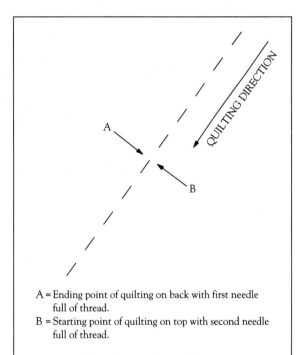

A = Ending point of quilting on back with first needle full of thread.

B = Starting point of quilting on top with second needle full of thread.

Point A and Point B are in the same location.

With this ending technique, it is possible to go beyond your quilting design to make the knot. This is possible because once the knot is made and pulled through to the batting layer, no stitch is visible in the area on top where the knot was made.

This technique has double security because of the knot and the extra thread beyond the knot buried in the batting. In the unlikely event that the knot should ever reappear on the top of the quilt, just fish out the extra thread, thread it on a needle, and re-bury it.

As mentioned earlier, there are many ways of starting and ending a line of quilting in addition to what is recommended above. And, although I believe my methods are undetectable and provide the best security, some of these other methods of starting and ending are also acceptable. But still other ways are unacceptable and are best avoided, such as duplicate stitches and backstitches. With duplicate stitches, each of the final five or six stitches is re-stitched in the opposite direction. This makes for messy, very obvious stitches that call attention to themselves. With backstitches at the beginning and ending of a line of quilting, the twist of the thread on the backstitches is the opposite of the twist of the thread on all of the other stitches, again calling undue attention to these stitches. The overall integrated look of a project demands that the entire work be in harmony without any jarring notes, so it's important that the starting and ending of the quilting lines be as unobtrusive as possible.

Practice the above outlined methods of starting a line of quilting, quilting the line, ending the line of quilting and getting even, small stitches. The results should repay your care and your practice. You will produce quilting that will please you as much as it will please others who see your finished work.

QUILTING EXERCISES

By now, you know what types of materials and tools to use, how to work with a quilting design, and how to execute the quilting stitch. However, no amount of reading can substitute for experience, so at this point it is time to put this information into practice on a series of exercises.

I realize, of course, that since you're not sitting in one of my workshops, I can't be sure you'll do the exercises. You could be saying, "Oh, I know what she means and I'll remember when I quilt – tomorrow." Take my word for it, you won't remember unless you experience each of the problems specifically in a practice situation. Doing the exercises will make your fingers remember, which will help your mind remember. So just pretend you're sitting in my workshop and try the exercises.

For the exercises, use a good grade of muslin for the top and backing of the textile sandwich and whichever type of batting, needle and quilting thread you prefer. Use any color of quilting thread that will contrast sharply with the muslin. Don't use white or off-white quilting thread. These are exercises so you want to be able to see every stitch clearly. Prewash, dry, and press the muslin; then cut the muslin and batting into squares. If you intend to work in a hoop or on a small frame, be sure to cut the fabric and batting large enough that they can to be held in place by the hoop or frame.

Mark each of the exercises on a separate piece of fabric. Remember that in all cases the arrow indicates the straight grain of the fabric. Assemble the textile sandwiches, being sure that the straight grain of the backing fabric is parallel to the straight grain of the top fabric and baste. Then, keeping in mind all of the factors discussed earlier, quilt the exercise projects. To refresh your memory on the problems inherent in each of the exercises, turn to the chapter which discusses working with the quilting design and reread the appropriate section before beginning the exercise.

While working on the specific problem in each exercise, be sure to also practice the starting and ending techniques and work hard to make all of the stitches and spaces on the top and back even.

To keep the information learned in mind, ensure that your completed exercises are visible at all times. Bind each of the exercises and hang them in your studio, sewing room, or whatever room in which you do your quiltmaking. Don't worry that they aren't perfect; they are practice pieces, places to get all the problems and mistakes out of your system so you won't have to deal with them when working on your quilt treasures.

QUILTING EXERCISES

EXERCISE A:
Straight grain quilting of parallel lines.

EXERCISE B:
Cross grain quilting of parallel lines.

EXERCISE C:
Bias quilting of parallel lines.

EXERCISE D:
Quilting curves.

EXERCISE E:
Quilting a continuous curve.

EXERCISE F:
Quilting multiple parallel curves.

EXERCISE G:
Quilting points and corners.

EXERCISE H:
Quilting across previously quilted lines.

EXERCISE I:
Quilting straight lines straight and
curved lines curved.

EXERCISE J:
Quilting circles.

EXERCISE K:
Quilting concentric circles.

QUILTING EXERCISE A

Straight grain quilting of parallel lines

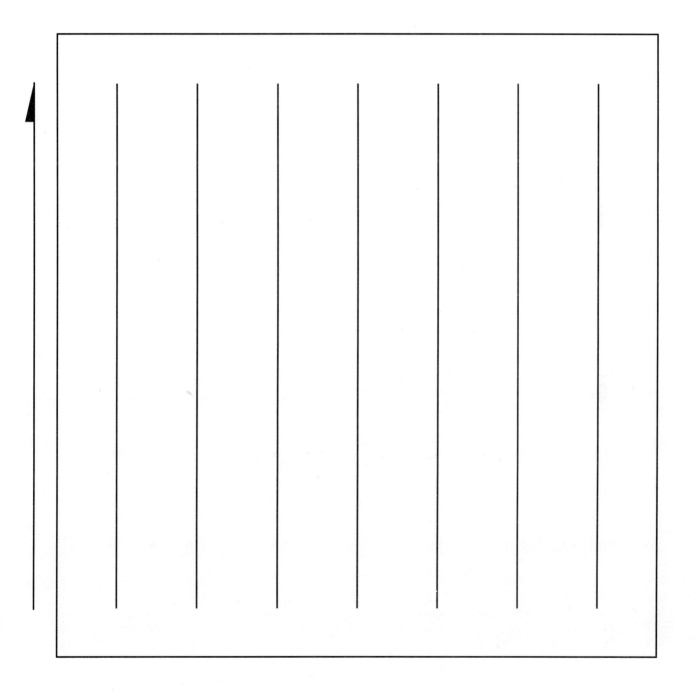

QUILTING EXERCISE B

Cross grain quilting of parallel lines

QUILTING EXERCISE C
Bias quilting of parallel lines

QUILTING EXERCISE D
Quilting curves

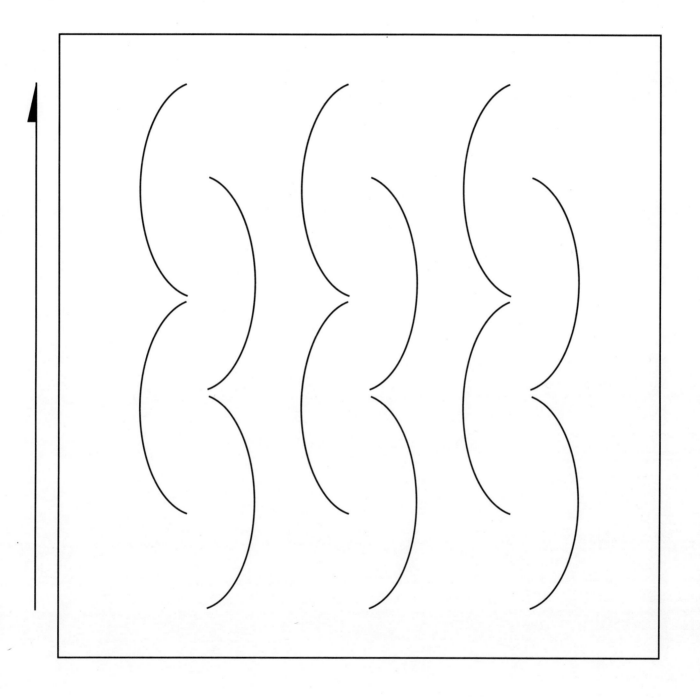

QUILTING EXERCISE E

Quilting a continuous curve

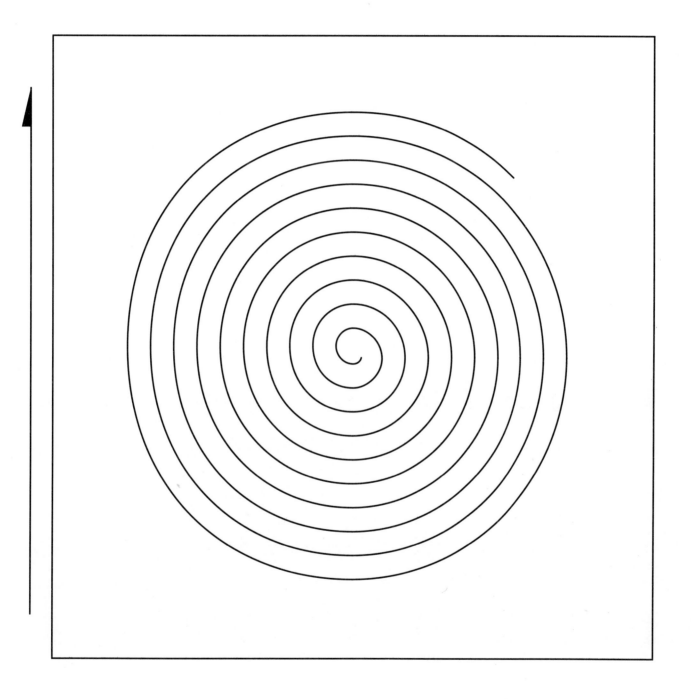

QUILTING EXERCISE F

Quilting multiple parallel curves

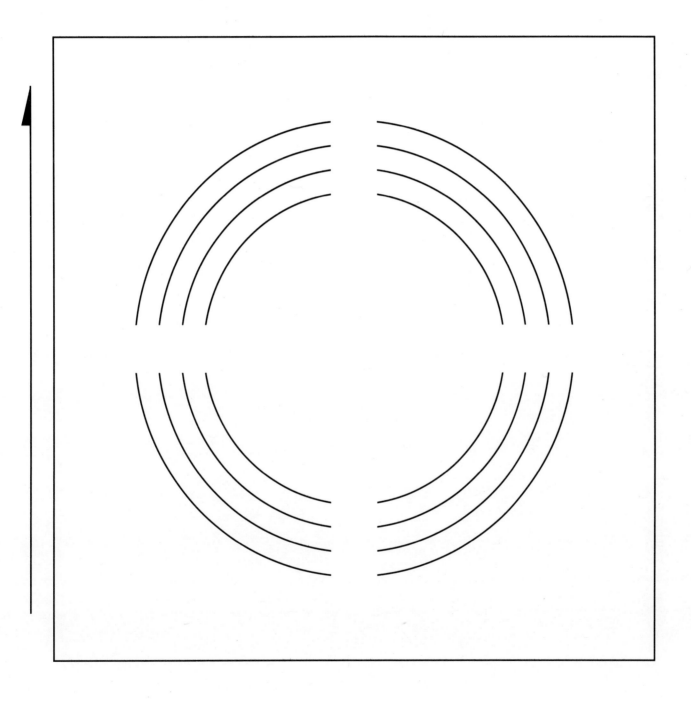

QUILTING EXERCISE G

Quilting points and corners

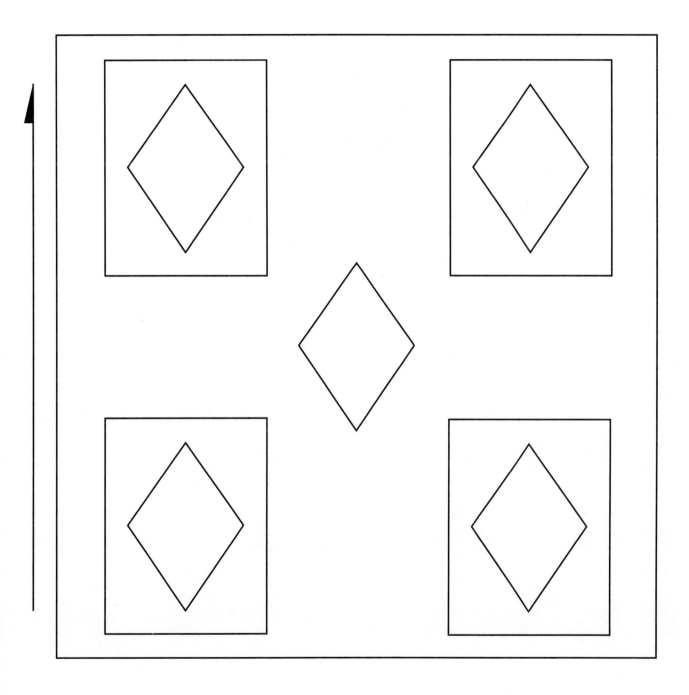

QUILTING EXERCISE H

Quilting across previously quilted lines

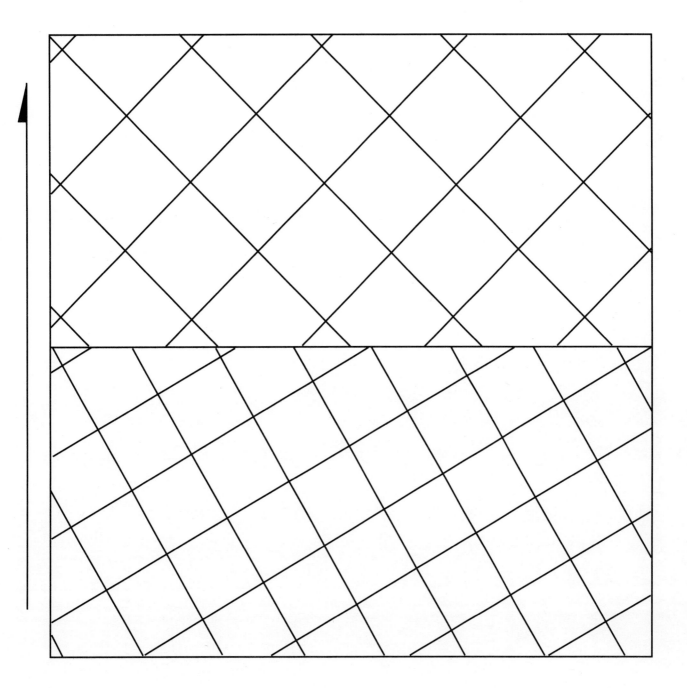

QUILTING EXERCISE I

Quilting straight lines straight and curved lines curved

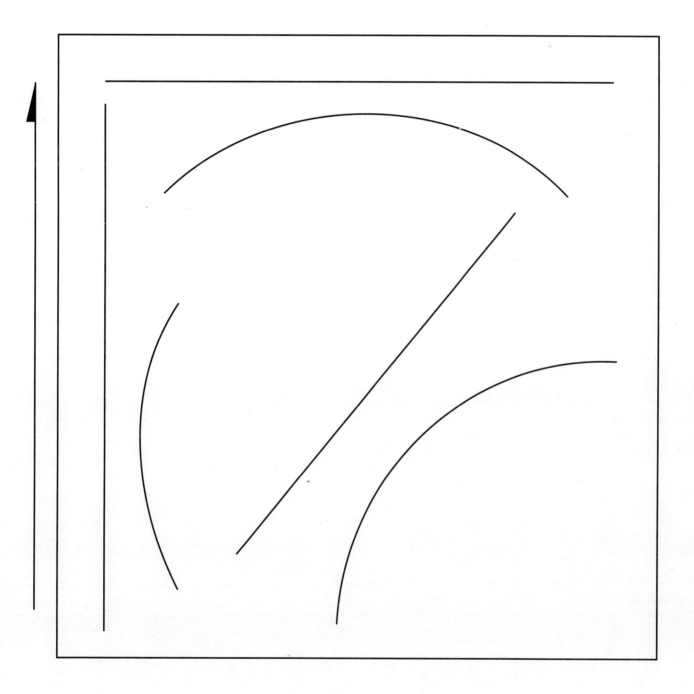

QUILTING EXERCISE J
Quilting circles

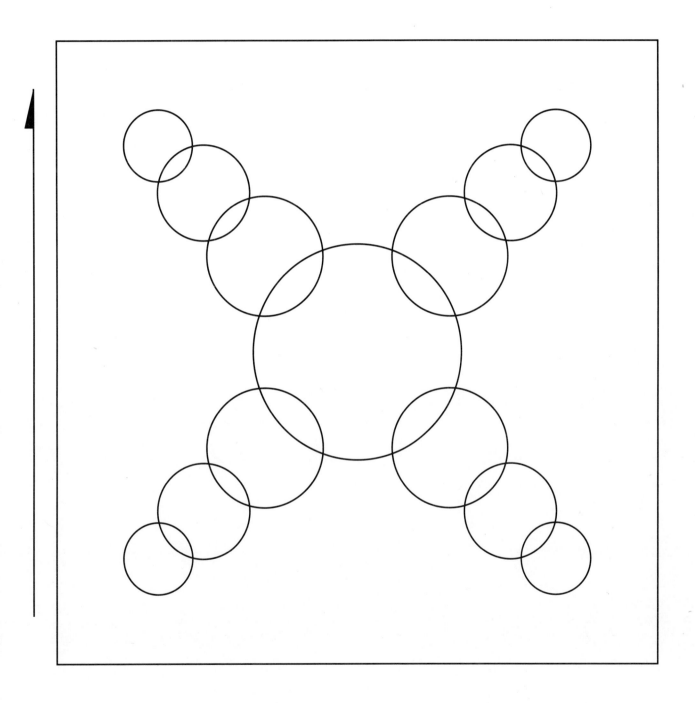

QUILTING EXERCISE K

Quilting concentric circles

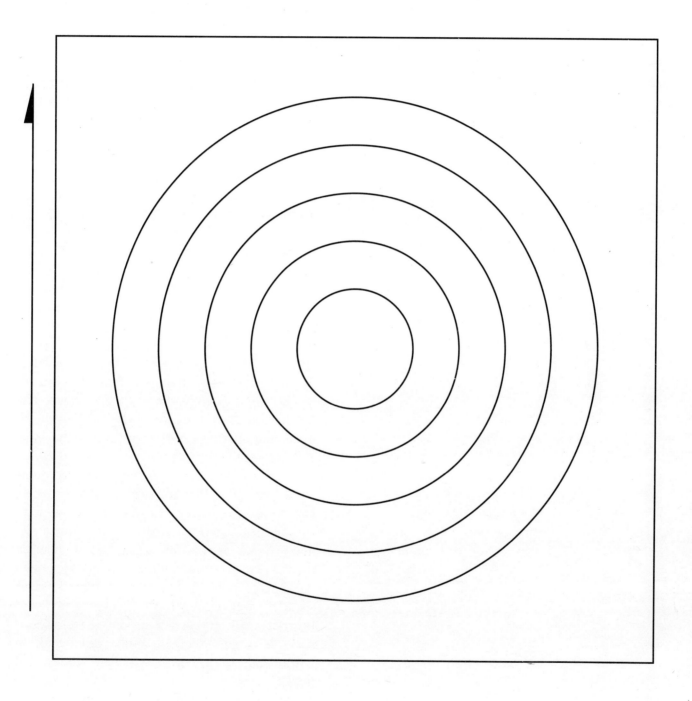

OTHER QUILTING STITCHES

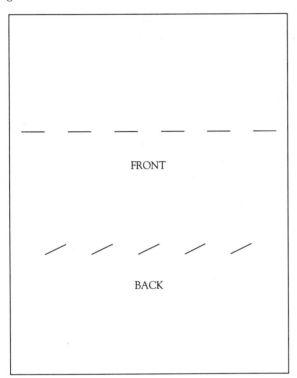

Fig. 58

FRONT

BACK

With the information you have so far, you are all set to quilt. Perhaps. Perhaps? Is there more to do? Yes, for while it may seem that a stitch is just a stitch, there are various types of stitches that are used by quilters. Some are effective and recommended and others should be avoided. Understanding all these types of stitches can add to your quilting effectiveness.

The running stitch is the one most commonly used for quilting. It is the simplest to stitch and the easiest to control. Using it is also the fastest way to quilt. The running stitch gives an overall uniform look to the quilting.

Some quilters prefer to quilt with a stab stitch. With the stab stitch, the needle is inserted into the top of the quilt, and is then pulled entirely through all three layers and out the back of the quilt. The needle is then inserted in the back of the quilt and pulled entirely through all three layers and back out the top. The stab stitch is difficult to control. Most often, when a stab stitch is used, the stitches on the top of the quilt will be straight while the stitches on the bottom of the quilt will be slanted (Fig. 58).

The stab stitch is also quite time consuming to execute. It may occasionally be necessary to use the stab stitch in conjunction with the running stitch when you are quilting across many thick seam allowances. Also, it may be used when you are quilting on an appliqued piece, especially in the area of turned under seam allowances when the background fabric has not been trimmed away. Some individuals are able to get excellent results when quilting with a stab stitch, but these people are few and far between.

Stipple quilting is the execution of a great many small stitches in extremely close rows or in an irregular pattern over an entire area. It is most often used in a background area to highlight the design in that area. Stipple quilting is both effective and time consuming. Generally, it is more effective when used sparingly.

Invisible quilting is a technique used by some individuals when quilting a commercial kit. A tiny stitch is made at each dot printed on the quilt top, then the quilter travels through the batting layer to the next dot where another tiny stitch is made, and so on. This is not really quilting at all and is unacceptable as a quilting technique because it neither satisfactorily holds the three layers together nor provides an additional design element to the work.

By the same token, when quilting on a kit, stitches should not be made to show the progress from dot to dot. In other words, don't come up at one dot, down at the next, up at the third and so forth. The resulting stitches and spaces are too large to effectively hold the layers so that they will not shift, and visually such stitches detract from the quilt. Those dots on a kit top are really taking the place of a solid line and you quilt along them just as you would any other marked quilting line.

Occasionally, you see a project quilted with a backstitch but this is a technique that is also unacceptable. It is time consuming and uses an extraordinarily large amount of thread. But the biggest objection is that even if the stitches on top are quite small, the stitches on the back are quite long and as such detract from the work (and could easily be caught or snagged during the life and use of the project).

I recommend starting with the running stitch and working to perfect it. The running stitch does the job of quilting effectively and relatively fast. It isn't mastered overnight, but with practice it can be developed into work you can be pleased with and proud of.

Other types of specialty quilting stitches can be effective and would be good areas for study once the traditional quilting stitch has been perfected.

UNBASTING

Once all of the quilting is complete, it is time to remove all of the basting stitches. Don't just pull the basting stitches out – they may have been caught by the quilting stitches so that pulling the basting could damage the quilting stitches. Forget even thinking about "taking out the basting" and think about "unbasting." Obviously, if you baste by putting in one stitch at a time, working from the center outward, you reverse the process for unbasting. To unbaste, remove one basting stitch at a time working from the outside toward the center. A convenient tool for this process is a rather large, blunt-ended tapestry needle. It will slip easily under the basting stitches without picking up any threads of the fabrics. The eye end of a regular needle is also an acceptable tool, but it is more difficult to handle than the larger tapestry needle.

If you find that a basting thread has been stitched through (caught) by the quilting, clip the basting thread at the place it is caught and proceed. Be sure to clip the basting thread, not the quilting stitch. Also, be very careful not to clip the fabric of the quilt top or backing. Work slowly and carefully while unbasting. Short and to the point: unbaste from stitch to stitch.

VARIABLES

Earlier, I discussed design, fabric, batting, thread, needles, marking tools and working methods that can all affect, or seem to affect, the quality of the quilting stitch. There are, however, other variables outside the quiltmaking realm that can affect the quality of the quilting.

It is vitally important to quilt only under optimum lighting conditions. Some individuals prefer to quilt only in natural light, while others prefer to quilt only in artificial light. I find it difficult to do any handwork in natural light because of the glare factor, so I work exclusively under artificial light. This takes us back to my thesis that you need to experiment for yourself to find, in this case, which lighting conditions work best.

Surprisingly, the temperature of the room in which you are working is important. If the room is too cold, it can affect the mobility of your fingers. If the room is too hot, you may perspire and your fingers will be slippery or sticky. High humidity can cause the same problems as a too hot room. A dry climate may cause your fingers to crack and bleed. If this happens, use a hand lotion that will be quickly and completely absorbed. Be sure there is no excess lotion left on your hands that could be transferred to the quilt when you begin quilting.

Whatever method you choose to use for quilting, whether in your hands, in a frame, or in a hoop, be certain that your chair provides proper support and is comfortable. Also, get up every forty-five minutes or so and go for a walk through the house and then return to your quilting. This will provide needed exercise and rest for your eyes; at the same time it won't take so long that you will lose your optimum quilting rhythm.

And speaking of your optimum quilting rhythm, constant interruptions will upset this rhythm and cause inconsistency in the quality of the work. Try to schedule your quilting sessions for times when you know that interruptions will be at a minimum. Many quilters get up early and quilt before the rest of the household stirs. If you are an early bird, this could be the answer for you. Other quilters prefer to work during the day when the family is at work or school, or the small ones are napping. Still other quilters prefer the late night hours after the rest of the family has retired. Study your typical week and pinpoint the times when you can best quilt uninterrupted. If your best plans for a quiet quilting period fall apart on any given day or interruptions become too frequent, give up quilting for that time slot and do some piecing or applique work. This type of work is not so adversely affected by interruptions.

Don't force yourself to quilt if you're not feeling well because the resultant work may reflect this. Quilting done when you have a headache or are suffering with the flu can wind up looking as if it were quilted by someone with a headache or the flu. I quilted a block once when I had a sprained left wrist. I was determined to finish it and, as I'm right-handed, I figured I could manage all right. Guess what – it looked as if had been quilted by someone with a sprained left wrist. Or at least by someone who was not doing a good job of controlling the stitches.

The flip side of this particular coin is not to quilt for such a long period of time that you adversely affect your health. You can wind up with "Quilter's Elbow," eyestrain, and muscle spasms. Remember to take a walk around the house regularly to help prevent these maladies. If you're an outdoor person, you can literally "walk around the house."

Your emotional state can have quite an effect on your quilting stitches. If you are upset or anxious about something, it can show in your work. At times like that, it's best to quilt on a small project or a practice piece rather than on a treasure. If you are in a calm emotional state, you'll find that the quilting goes more easily and you will be able to produce some of your best work.

By the same token, your quilting can affect your emotional state. If the fabrics are difficult to work with, if the thread keeps fraying, you can find yourself becoming terribly aggravated by the entire project. That's when you need to walk away from it and do something else for a while. But you will also find that quilting can be calming and relaxing and have a soothing effect on you as the quilter. If you are upset or having a sleepless night, try quilting for a while (on a practice piece or small project) and you'll usually find yourself in a much better frame of mind as the rhythmic stitching becomes automatic and the pleasing design grows beneath your hands.

Whenever possible, avoid quilting under tight deadlines. A quilting job rushed to completion will frequently result in a quilted project that looks as if it was done in a hurry. You will probably reduce the amount of quilting you originally planned, and the quality of the quilting stitches will suffer. Now, it is reasonable to set some deadlines for yourself or you'll probably never get a project completed. But just be sure that any deadlines you set are realistic and allow some margin for the unexpected. You know you'll enjoy your completed project, but it's just as important, and for some maybe more important, to enjoy the quilting while you're doing it. Tight deadlines do not allow for much enjoyment in the doing of the work.

DIAGNOSING PROBLEMS

Sometimes quilters are relatively pleased with their quilting stitches, but are having one or another small problem that keeps them from being completely satisfied with their work. In order to eliminate these problems, it is first necessary to find out what is causing them.

In this chapter you will find some of the most common problems that quilters run into and how to deal with them. In some cases you should be reminded of information presented earlier in this book.

Knot won't pop through the backing or breaks while you're trying to pop it through.

Knot is probably too large. Try again with a smaller knot.

Knot pops through the backing, though the batting, and then out through the top.

Knot is probably too small. Try again with a larger knot.

Stitches on the back are much too small.

Hold the needle in a much more vertical position on the downward stroke of the stitch. For severe cases, you might even consider pointing the needle backwards very slightly on the downward stroke.

Stitches on the top are tiny but the spaces are big.

Enlarge the top stitches until they are the same size as the spaces. Quilt with these even stitches and spaces. After you have developed an even stitch, work toward reducing the size of both stitches and spaces at the same time.

Top is pulled slightly between parallel rows of quilting.

Quilt all the parallel rows in the same direction instead of quilting down one row and up the next.

Amount of puff between rows of quilting varies.

If you're working on a frame or hoop, tighten the tension of the piece. If you are quilting in your hands, keep your hands and fingers still. Don't shove the fabric toward the needle. Also, if you are working in your hands, be sure you are quilting toward your holding hand.

Straight quilted lines are not straight after all.

If you're working on a frame or hoop, be sure the line is straight before starting to quilt. If you're quilting in your hands, work toward your holding hand, not parallel to it.

Skipped stitches on the back.

Check the area you're quilting. If you're losing stitches as you move between the straight or cross grains and the bias, listen carefully as you quilt. You will hear these stitches drop off the needle. Don't bring the needle back up until you've redone the stitch(es) on the back.

Little "x's" or "+'s" appear all over the quilted background grid.

Gauge your stitches so you are crossing a previously quilted line on the back of the quilt instead of on the front.

Quilting is done with one large stitch followed by two small stitches then another large stitch and two small stitches all along.

You are putting three stitches on the needle at one time and not gauging them accurately. Try putting two or four stitches on the needle at a time. If this doesn't work, try looking at the stitches on the needle and being sure the stitches and spaces line up on the needle are the same size before pulling the needle through. And, if this doesn't work, do one stitch at a time. This will usually cure the problem when all else fails, and even though you may feel it takes more time, it will be worth it to get the stitches even.

The quilting stitches look like basting stitches.

Reduce the size of the stitches and spaces while quilting.

The stitches lie loosely on top of the quilt.

Pull the stitches more tightly so they are actively holding the three layers together.

The stitches seem to almost cause gathers on the quilt.

Adjust the tension of the stitches so you are not pulling them so tightly.

After quilting is completed, the piece doesn't lie flat and the sides are not straight.

Possibly the amount of quilting differs widely from one area to another, especially if it is a sampler, medallion or pictorial quilt. Additional quilting in the sparsely quilted areas may help relieve this somewhat.

The project is extremely difficult to quilt.

Most likely the problem is caused by the fabric or batting and it's too late to do anything about it at this point. Persevere, and next time be sure both the fabric and the batting needle well before incorporating them into a project.

Contrasting color quilting thread is calling too much attention to the quilting stitches at the expense of the quilt top design.

Switch to a color of quilting thread that matches or comes close to matching the color of the fabric.

Marking is still visible after quilting is completed.

Remove all the marks (See "Marking Tools"). Next time, use another method of marking that will not create this problem.

Bubbles or pleats are being quilted into the backing fabric.

Add more basting or re-baste entirely. Also, put the project more tightly in the hoop or frame or hold it more firmly in your hands.

Stitches at points and corners are pulled slightly sideways.

Concentrate on gauging your stitches so you are coming up and not going down at a point or corner.

The first and last stitch of every line of quilting stick out like sore thumbs.

Don't start and stop the lines of quilting with a backstitch.

Blood spots on the quilt.

Use cold water or (sorry about this indelicacy) saliva to remove them immediately. In the future, protect your fingers while quilting.

Traveling stitches in the batting layer are visible through the quilt top.

Travel more deeply in the batting layer.

Traveling stitches are on the back of the quilt.

Travel only in the batting layer and never on the back or the front of the quilt.

Broken or pulled quilting stitches.

Remember to unbaste carefully.

If you've come up with an entirely different problem not covered in the preceding pages, concentrate on watching your fingers while you quilt and you will probably be able to determine the cause of the problem for yourself. Once you know the cause of it, work carefully to develop a working technique that will eliminate the problem. If you can't spot what you're doing to cause the problem, ask a quilting friend to watch you quilt and help you figure it out.

You will find quilting more enjoyable if the work is not a series of problems and aggravations. It's worth making the effort to correct any problems you may be having so your quilted project will be the best work of which you are capable.

FINISHING

There are any number of acceptable methods for finishing the edges of your quilt. The first guiding factor when choosing a finishing method is to be sure that it is compatible with the top design and that it enhances rather than detracts from it. Actually, the method you choose, as long as it's compatible with the top design, is probably not as important as how well you execute it.

There are some general guidelines to keep in mind when finishing the quilt edges. First, be sure that the batting completely and evenly fills the edges. Don't have thin areas where the batting doesn't extend all the way to the edge. If necessary add narrow strips of batting to fill these edges. And, if there is excess batting, don't just fold it over and leave it there or you'll have a thick spot. Trim it back evenly.

It is important that the color of thread used for the finishing match the color of the fabric used. The finishing should not call attention to itself by having unmatched thread color. The stitches that are used for finishing should be small, tight, and close together.

At some point in the finishing process, it is important to be sure to sign and date your work. It's also a good idea to include the title of the work along with the signature and the date. If your quilt doesn't have a title, you might consider including the pattern name.

There are various ways to sign and date your work. The information can be quilted into the work or it can be embroidered on the work. Waste canvas can be used and results in a tidy and readable signature. A label can be stitched onto the back of the quilt. The label could be embroidered, cross-stitched, typed, handwritten or you could use one of the commercial labels available on today's market.

I prefer that the signature and date be a part of the quilt so I embroider it on, usually using a whipped backstitch, but quilting it in or using waste canvas would also answer my requirement. A label stitched to the quilt would definitely be a second choice but infinitely better than not including the information.

When my down-the-line descendants inherit my work in the middle of the 21st century, they won't need to wonder who did it – my name will be there. I figure that's the least I can do for them and for future quilt historians.

AFTERWORD

Piecing, applique and quilting are the three basic techniques associated with the art of quiltmaking. Of these, I feel the most important technique is quilting. It is the one technique that can stand alone. You can make a whole-cloth quilt using only quilting stitches and when you are finished, you have a quilt. This isn't true of piecing or applique. Once you do the piecing or applique work, you still have to quilt it before it is a completed work. Quilting is the technique that is the *sine qua non* of quiltmaking.

When quilting is added to the pieced or appliqued work, it truly makes the quilt, bringing it to life and giving it a full practical or decorative life of its own. It follows, then, that it's necessary to perfect the quilting stitch. In order to perfect it, the first thing is to seriously want to do a better job of quilting and then to concentrate on working out any problems that exist. It's important to identify and eliminate any bad habits and to develop good habits that will lead to good quilting.

In my frame of reference, it's not enough to persevere through the quilting simply to get a project completed. I think it is absolutely vital to derive enjoyment from the work while doing it. If it isn't pleasurable or if it is a constant source of aggravation, I stop doing it. The best way to make it a pleasure and to eliminate irritations is to master the quilting technique. Being confident about what you are doing and being satisfied with the results you are getting is where one gets enjoyment out of quilting.

Watching other people quilt and learning all you can from every quiltmaker and every quilting information source will help make you a better quiltmaker. Remember, it's true that you should take time as you go through life to smell the roses. By the same token, take time to enjoy your quilting, both after the project is completed and while you are working on it.

Happy Stitches!

APPENDIX: SELECTED QUILTING PATTERN BOOKS

Bailey, Kay. *Quilting Stitchery, No. 1.* Maple Plain, MN: Homeart, 1978.

---------- *Quilting Stitchery, No. 2.* Maple Plain, MN: Homeart, 1981.

---------- *Quilting Stitchery, No. 3.* Maple Plain, MN: Homeart, 1983.

Cory, Pepper. *Quilting Designs From Antique Quilts.* Lafayette, CA: C & T Publishing, 1987.

---------- *Quilting Designs From the Amish.* Lafayette, CA: C & T Publishing, 1985.

Cox, Patricia. *Every Stitch Counts.* Minneapolis, MN: One of a Kind Quilting Design, 1981.

Emery, Linda Goodmon. *A Treasury of Quilting Designs.* Paducah, KY: American Quilter's Society, 1990.

Fons, Marianne. *Fine Feathers.* Lafayette, CA: C & T Publishing, 1988.

Handful O' Hearts, Book 1. Chicago, IL: The Contemporary Quilt, 1982.

Inglis, Charlotte. *Making Your Own Custom Quilting Stencils.* Dexter, MI: Inglis Publications, 1981.

Johnson, Mary Alice. *Quilting Designs for Miniatures, Blocks & Borders.* Castroville, CA: Privately published, n.d.

Leathers, Millie and Marquerite Wiebusch. *Stitching a Legacy, Designs for Quilting, Book 1.* Russiaville, IN: Calico Pedlars Press, 1981.

Lindsey, Linda. *Design for Quilting and Needle Arts.* Monmouth, OR: Privately published, 1980.

----------. *More Designs for Quilting and Needle Arts.* Monmouth, OR: Privately published, 1984.

Macho, Linda. *Quilting Patterns.* NY: Dover Publications, Inc., 1984.

Miller, Denise Oyama and Kaaren Tajnak. *Quilting Designs, Volume 1.* Fremont, CA: Bear's Paw Press, 1980.

Neff, Loraine. *Original Quilting Designs.* Paducah, KY: American Quilter's Society, 1985.

Robertson, Virginia. *Miniature Quilting Designs.* Overbrook, KS: The Osage County Quilt Factory, 1988.

Squire, Helen. *Ask Helen ... More About Quilting Designs.* Paducah, KY: American Quilter's Society, 1990.

---------- *Dear Helen, Can You Tell Me?* Paducah, KY: American Quilter's Society, 1987.

Szalavary, Anne. *Decorative Quilting Patterns.* NY: Dover Publications, Inc.; 1989.

Thompson, Shirley. *The Finishing Touch.* Edmonds, WA: Powell Publications, 1980.

---------- *It's Not a Quilt Until It's Quilted.* Edmonds, WA: Powell Publications, 1984.

---------- *Old-Time Quilting Designs.* Edmonds, WA: Powell Publications, 1988.

---------- *Tried & True.* Edmonds, WA: Powell Publications, 1987.

Traditional Feather Wreaths, Book 2. Chicago, IL: The Contemporary Quilt, 1982.

Tribuno, Bertha Reth. *The Miniature Whole-Cloth Quilt Collection.* Cedar Rapids, IA: Heritage Quilting Designs, 1988.

Vale, Dianna. *New Stitches, Original Quilting Designs.* Salem, OR: Privately published, 1979.

---------- *New Stitches, Book II.* Salem, OR: Privately published, 1981.

---------- *New Stitches, Book III.* Salem, OR: Privately published, 1982.

---------- *New Stitches, Book IV.* Salem, OR: Privately published, 1984.

----------. *New Stitches, Book V.* Salem, OR: Privately published, 1986.

Wiebusch, Marguerite. *More Feathers and Other Fancies.* Russiaville, IN: Privately published, 1984.

Wright, Sharon. *"White on White."* Jenison, MI: Honey Bee Publications, 1985.